Why
Scottish
Philosophy
Matters

Alexander Broadie

THE SALTIRE SOCIETY

Why Scottish Philosophy Matters
published 2000 by
The Saltire Society
9 Fountain Close,
22 High Street,
Edinburgh EH1 1TF

A catalogue record for this book is available
from the British Library.

ISBN 0 85411 075 5

The Publisher acknowledges the financial support of the
Scottish Arts Council towards the publication of this book.

Cover Design by James Hutcheson

Printed and bound in Scotland by Bell & Bain Limited

Contents

Preface

Scottish philosophy matters to Scotland and to philosophy, and on both counts it matters to me. That it matters to Scotland is demonstrated by the centrality of the position that it has occupied through the centuries in the high culture of Scotland. That it matters to philosophy is demonstrated by the immensity of its contribution to the western philosophical tradition, a tradition in which thinkers such as John Duns Scotus and David Hume are universally recognised for the universal significance of their insights.

The Scottish philosophical tradition is extraordinarily rich and my chief problem in writing this book has concerned the hard choices that have had to be made. Many who contributed to the tradition and whose works are widely read beyond as well as within Scotland have not even been mentioned here. Among them are some of my own favourites, but sadly I cannot include one person's favourites without excluding somebody else's. Many topics also have been omitted, but the few that have been included form a tight-knit system and have been prominent in Scottish philosophy down the centuries. That tight-knit system is central to what I believe to be *the* Scottish philosophy, a distinct, strong voice heard in this country since medieval times, and still to be heard, loud and clear – for it has not yet run its course. This book is written from within that philosophical tradition and aims to be a contribution to debates within it, rather than to be no more than a historical account. The book is therefore a work of philosophy as well as of history, and the history is for the sake of the philosophy.

Philosophy and writing books are both, though in different ways, social activities. *Why Scottish Philosophy Matters* is exemplary in this respect. It has benefited from help generously given by Misericòrdia Anglès and Patricia S. Martin, and I am grateful to them.

A.B.
Glasgow
April 1999

CHAPTER 1

Introduction

I do not take lightly the title of this book. I believe that Scottish philosophy matters greatly and my principal aim is to say why it matters. This task cannot be accomplished in the first paragraph, or even in the first chapter. Two preliminary questions must be tackled, for it is necessary for me to say, first, why I think that there is such a thing as Scottish philosophy, and secondly, what I think it is. I have a clear idea, clear at any rate to me, what the answers are to these questions, and the greater part of the book will be taken up with providing them. Only when that is done, and we are poised before the final chapter, will we be well placed to deal with the question posed in the title. Up to the last chapter therefore the book is a work of philosophy, and whatever there is of value in the final chapter derives from the value of the preceding discussions.

The book is by no means a historical survey of Scottish philosophy, a breathless scamper through eight centuries from the High Middle Ages up to the present. Nevertheless the history of Scottish philosophy is at the centre of my story, for I have focused upon three moments in that history, from the High Middle Ages, the pre-Reformation period, and the Enlightenment, moments that fall, approximately, in the thirteenth, the sixteenth and the eighteenth centuries. The discussions of the pre-Enlightenment, indeed of the pre-Reformation, period occupy the greater part of this book; and given the dominant position of the philosophy of the Scottish Enlightenment in the public's knowledge of Scottish philosophy, the considerable space that I have devoted to the earlier period calls for justification. If Scottish philosophy in the Age of Enlightenment is overwhelmingly the best and most important philosophy that we have produced then why does this book not focus overwhelmingly on that period? I have four reasons for my choice.

First, the fact that even the names of almost all the pre-Reformation Scottish philosophers are unknown to a philosophically literate public, such as is the Scottish public, calls for redress. Perhaps the only one whose name is at all widely known is John Duns Scotus, but there is a wide chasm between knowing his name and knowing his philosophy. Nor is his name at all worth knowing except as associated with the wonderful system of thought that he conjured up. In the following pages I try to convey a sense of the depth of his thinking. But there are other pre-Reformation Scottish philosophers, and it is important that their ideas also be placed in the public domain, even if only to allow the public to judge whether their writings have merit. Of course, I think their writings are full of good things. But first it is necessary for me, and not merely out of considerations of politeness, to introduce those whom I believe to be key figures. As to whether their writings matter, in the final chapter I shall seek to argue that they do. But I hope that by then I shall hardly need to argue the case.

Secondly, I aim to demonstrate that there is a tradition of philosophy in this country, a tradition with a distinctive content. I am not speaking here simply about the philosophy of the Enlightenment, though the distinctive content I have in mind is brilliantly represented in the Scottish Enlightenment. But the point that has to be emphasised is that there is a very long tradition, one that can be traced back to the High Middle Ages. From the point of view of the thesis of this book, the earlier the date of anchorage the better, and it is easy to trace it to the twelfth century, though in fact my detailed story will begin in the thirteenth.

Thirdly, my purpose is not merely to say that the Scottish philosophical tradition is very long indeed, but to emphasise the continuity of a particular philosophical content. As just stated, that content surfaced in the eighteenth century, and my detailed consideration of earlier periods of the tradition can be treated in part as a scene-setting exercise, the provision of a context that allows deeper insight into what actually happened of philosophical importance in the Enlightenment in Scotland.

Fourthly, I aim to emphasise that Scottish philosophy not merely existed before the Enlightenment but flourished, and indeed flourished no less than during the Enlightenment itself. Pre-Reformation Scottish philosophy represents one of the great triumphs of Scottish culture.

Why then is that philosophy such a well-kept secret? There are at least two reasons, neither of them quite straightforward. The first relates to language. During the pre-Reformation period almost all Scottish works with a substantial philosophical content were written in Latin, and only a very small fraction of those writings have been translated into English. Of course, that explains why today very few read the works in question. But even in the latter part of the sixteenth century few in this country were reading those works although Latin was then a much more common accomplishment. However, it has to be recalled that the sixteenth century was the great age of return to the classical languages, Latin, Greek and Hebrew. Latin was of course the normal language of scholarly discourse in the Middle Ages, but the Latin of the sixteenth century humanists was very different. It was, as far as could be managed in the sixteenth century, the Latin of the great historians, orators and poets of ancient Rome. On the other hand the pre-Reformation Scottish philosophers wrote a Latin that would have been barely, if at all, intelligible to Cicero. In Scotland from the middle of the sixteenth century there was little or no sympathy for the Latin of the Middle Ages as the scholars of that later century struggled to emulate the style of the great writers of Rome.

The second reason the philosophy of the pre-Reformation period is so well-kept a secret relates to the fact of the Reformation itself. It is often said that history is written by the victors and, though the dictum exaggerates, it contains a significant measure of truth. Almost all Scottish philosophy of the earlier period was written by men who belonged to the priesthood of what came to be a discredited Church. To whomsoever the Scottish philosophers of subsequent generations might turn for philosophical inspiration it could not be to thinkers upon whom the country as a whole had turned its back when the Reformation came to Scotland around 1560. The history of philosophy, as the subject was subsequently taught in Scottish universities, focused on the writers of Greece and Rome and then leapt foward to the post-Reformation period, as if nothing much of note had happened in philosophy for more than a millennium. In that sense the victors in Scotland's sixteenth-century religious revolution dictated the history of philosophy. And, on the whole, the history they dictated is still accepted.

Nevertheless, however deep the religious divide may have been, and may be even now, even deeper down the divisions melt away. I believe that there is a fundamental stance, the same fundamental stance, adopted by Scottish philosophers across the centuries and that it is as clearly present in the Enlightenment as in pre-Reformation times. I shall explore this stance in some detail. The fact of philosophical continuities prompts interesting questions relating to mechanisms of historical causation, but I shall have little to say here in answer to them. They are for someone who is not only a philosopher but also a historian – which I am not.

This book has been written for those who have asked themselves philosophical questions concerning us human beings and our place in the world, and have wondered what Scotland's contribution has been to debates on these questions of universal import. The good news is that Scotland's contribution has been, and has been universally recognised to be, immense. Further news, no less welcome, is that its contribution is accessible to all with a philosophical bent. That means all of us, for an ability to think philosophically is part of our human endowment – a part that is nowhere more conspicuous than here in Scotland.

CHAPTER 2

The Scottish Philosophical Tradition

The question 'Why does Scottish philosophy matter?' prompts the logically antecedent question whether there is such a thing as Scottish philosophy. One might give a negative answer to the latter question on the grounds that no country, nor therefore this one, has a philosophy. For philosophy is by its nature an activity which addresses questions of universal significance and does so in a way that makes an appeal equally to the rationality of all people and therefore makes its appeal independently of national characteristics or considerations. And if in philosophising a universal faculty speaks forth on matters of universal significance, then surely there cannot be such a thing as a 'national philosophy'. On an obvious understanding of this argument it seems sound, for philosophy is indeed by its nature universal. And if philosophy is properly characterised by its universality then, it seems, to nationalise philosophy is to destroy its nature, for nationality is a kind of singularity, and singularity is contrary to universality.

Nevertheless I believe there to be such a thing as Scottish philosophy. And I am encouraged to think that it is at least possible for it to exist, for philosophers themselves have no qualms about speaking of philosophy in nationalistic terms. For example, there are books on 'German philosophy', and 'post-Kantian German idealism' is a major field of study. Likewise there are many references to 'English empiricism', and so on. And having ruled in a German philosophy and an English one, it seems unfair to rule out *a priori* the possibility of a Scottish one. Furthermore there is no merit in seeking to argue that German idealism cannot really exist for there can be nothing German about the brand of philosophical idealism in question. The relevant point here is that philosophers have found the phrase 'German idealism' useful as a classificatory tool, and if philosophers have found it useful that seems a good reason not to jettison the phrase, least of all on philosophical grounds, since those who would appreciate the grounds best, philosophers themselves, clearly do not take those grounds seriously. Why should it not be, therefore, that the phrase 'Scottish philosophy' may also be found useful as a classificatory tool? And if it is, then there must be something that can be classified as Scottish philosophy. It remains to be demonstrated however that there is after all such a thing. It should be said at once that the task of finding it can be approached with confidence that Scottish philosophy exists, even if the route to the definition of it is difficult (as it is). For there are many references by philosophers, especially in the nineteenth century, to what they term 'Scottish philosophy'. There is no doubt that some of the thinkers who used the phrase, such as William Hamilton and James Ferrier, were certain that such a thing existed. However, though I believe them to be right, I do not answer the question 'What is Scottish philosophy?' quite as the nineteenth-century writers did, for I attach especial significance to a part of the story that those writers totally or almost totally ignored. The part in question is pre-Reformation.

In answering the question my focus, upon three salient moments in the history of philosophy, will be personalised by the linking of each moment to a particular philosopher. The first is John Duns Scotus (c.1266-1308) from the village of Duns in Berwickshire, the second John Mair (c.1467-1550) from Gleghornie near Haddington, and the third Thomas Reid (1710-96) from Strachan in Aberdeenshire. The three men are philosophically very closely linked. Mair had intimate knowledge of the writings of Scotus. Though, so far as I know, Reid never read Scotus, he did not need to; he worked out for himself the same ideas that Scotus likewise had worked out for himself. The outcome is that the spirit of Scotus appears to hover in ghostly attendance upon the thoughtful Reid. Scottish philosophy is of course much more than the systems of these great men; it is a vast and richly textured culture, a dialogue maintained across seven or eight centuries and, for much of that time, reaching deep down into the human spirit. But I believe that more than anyone else these innovative thinkers give substance to the concept of Scottish philosophy, somewhat as Thomas Aquinas gives substance to the concept of Christian philosophy and Aristotle gives substance to the concept of philosophy *simpliciter*.

Much of this book will consist of exposition and discussion of philosophical doctrines; it will, in short, be an account of what I take to be central features of Scottish philosophy, with a view to defining what is characteristically Scottish about the philosophy. Having offered the definition, space will thereby have been created within which it will be possible to give an answer, rooted in the Scottish philosophical tradition, to the question why Scottish philosophy matters, and especially why it is important that Scots should know their own philosophical heritage.

I believe Scotus to be Scotland's greatest philosopher and to have set down markers which have been present ever since in the philosophical life of Scotland. Yet there is a problem that has to be faced. Though Scotus was born in Scotland and throughout his days bore the name that declared this fact, he was taken from the country in his youth, at an age which is not recorded though it is reported that he had already received in Scotland a grounding in Latin grammar; and, so far as is known, once departed he never returned. If his birthplace is all that links him to Scotland why is it appropriate to think of him as a Scottish philosopher and as being part of the story of Scottish philosophy? Birthplace and name are surely not by themselves enough.

John Mair affirms that it was because at that time there existed no university in Scotland that Scotus was taken south to Oxford by two Scottish Franciscan friars. Scotus studied and taught at Oxford, and thereafter his teaching career took him also to Paris and to Cologne where he died and was buried. His itinerary is set forth in the inscription on his tomb in the Conventual Franciscan Church in

Cologne: *Scotia me genuit. Anglia me suscepit. Gallia me docuit. Colonia me tenet*: 'Scotland begot me. England reared me. France taught me. Cologne holds my remains.' Yet for all his travels, and though associated with four countries, he is identified with one only, the one that was his. On the seventh centenary of his birth the Franciscan Order erected a cairn in Duns. The plaque reads: 'John Duns Scotus, the Subtle Doctor, and member of the Franciscan Order, was born on this site in 1266. Wherever his distinguished name is uttered, he sheds lustre on Duns and Scotland, the town and land which bore him.'

There seems no reason to dispute John Mair's explanation of Scotus's departure from Scotland, the fact that this country did not at that time have a university. This lack meant that if it was thought that a child's intellectual talent should be nurtured he (I say 'he' advisedly) was likely to be taken furth of Scotland to continue his education. After Scotus's departure the two places at which he spent most time were Oxford and Paris, and almost all his extant works are, or are based on, lectures he delivered at these two great centres. But no-one claims him as an English or a French philosopher; his name of course would be enough to give pause to anyone who thought of making such a claim, but there is much more to it than that as I shall now demonstrate.

In 1411/1412 the University of St Andrews was founded, Scotland's first, to be followed in the same century by the universities of Glasgow (1451) and Aberdeen (1495). These were, in the early days, very small institutions as compared with the great centres of learning elsewhere, such as Oxford, Paris and Cologne, but within a very short period it became possible for Scots to be taught by Scots at as high a level as was available anywhere in Europe. Many Scots who had received their training abroad, especially at the University of Paris, and who had progressed to regentships and professorships at Paris, returned to the universities of Scotland, to form a phalanx of high-quality teachers. Others returned from these lofty positions and took up other roles in the country, where again they could set the educational tone of the country. One philosopher in the latter group was John Ireland (c.1440-95), a graduate of St Andrews, who then matriculated at the University of Paris, and rose to be that university's rector, briefly in 1469. John Ireland, who was Scotland's most important philosopher of the second half of the fifteenth century, and who had been confessor to James III, wrote a large prose work in Scots for James IV. The book, *The Mirror of Wisdom*, was intended, in part, as advice to the king regarding the duties of kingship. It is noticeable that in the *Mirror* Ireland keeps a respectful and friendly eye on Duns Scotus, *doctor subtilis*. He speaks of Scotus as 'Doctor Subtilis that was a great clerk of Paris and born of this land'. He then affirms that 'the doctor subtle in his *Book of the Sentences* in the Prologue induces eight manner of ways to prove and persuade the faith'. These eight ways are then expounded and discussed. Subsequently Ireland turns to questions concerning divine prescience and its relation to human freedom, and again he invokes Scotus.

In 1495, the year of John Ireland's death, James Liddell (Jacobus Ledelh), a regent in arts at the University of Paris, published a little *Treatise on Concepts and Signs*. Liddell is an important figure in the history of Scottish culture in general and of Scottish philosophy in particular. He was born in Aberdeen c.1460, and in 1483 graduated in arts at the University of Paris. He stayed on in Paris to teach, and in 1486 was appointed examiner to Scottish students in the University. 1495 saw the foundation of King's College in Liddell's home town. His *Treatise on Concepts and Signs*, a technical work on mental acts, has especial significance because it was the first ever book by a Scot that was printed in his own lifetime, for though the writings of other Scots, notably Duns Scotus, had been printed earlier, they were printed after the death of their authors. The *Treatise*, of which the sole extant copy is in the National Library of Scotland, is the best possible symbol of Scotland's status as a nation of philosophers. Liddell, who went on to practise medicine, died probably after 1519 and, as with Liddell himself, his book seems to have slipped into total oblivion. But the *Treatise* is worthy of a much kinder fate.

In 1495, the year of the publication of Liddell's book, John Mair became regent in arts at the University of Paris, and rose to become professor of theology. He also spent five years (1518-23) as principal of the University of Glasgow, and in addition taught for many years at St Andrews, where he was provost of St Salvator's College from 1534 till his death in 1550. At Paris Mair inspired great respect and affection among students and teachers alike. One of his students speaks of him as a deeply knowledgeable man whose virtue is as great as his faith, and another speaks of 'my master John Mair, the very eminent prince of theologians at Paris, and not only of theologians but of philosophers also, as all the arts in Paris have emanated from him as from an endlessly limpid and gushing spring'. Mair's lectures were heard by John Calvin, Ignatius Loyola, George Buchanan, François Rabelais, and many others among the great movers and shakers of that revolutionary century of religious reformation and renaissance humanism. He was in addition an immensely prolific man. Most of his works, if not all of them, are extant, and they cover an immense range. The passage referred to earlier, concerning the transference of Scotus from Scotland to Oxford, was taken from Mair's *History of Greater Britain*. In that same section of the book Mair is happy to include the detail that 'Duns Scotus, that subtle doctor... was born at Duns, a village eight miles distant from England, and separated from my own home by seven or eight leagues only'. In its context this piece of information is hardly relevant, but, having introduced Scotus to the reader, Mair's plain intention was to let the world see his pride in being associated, even by geographical proximity, with the great thinker.

It should be added that Mair shows his admiration for Scotus in many ways. For example he led a three-man editorial team which prepared an edition of Scotus's Commentary on the *Sentences of Peter Lombard*, a Commentary that Scotus based on a set of lectures he had given while at Paris. It is notable that throughout his career Mair wrote about Scotus, referring to him, not as 'Scotus' or as *doctor subtilis'* (his honorific title), but as *conterraneus* – my compatriot, a fellow Scot. I believe that this was not merely fellow feeling for a fellow Scot, or even for a fellow Scot who was also a philosopher and theologian who had spent an important part of his career in Paris – the parallels are impressive. It was fellow-feeling for a philosopher with whose system he could feel at home. Scotland was homeland for both men, and Scotus's system was an intellectual homeland for Mair. Mair was an independent thinker, his own man, but of course he was subject to influences, and he found the systems of some thinkers more congenial than others. He was for example strongly hostile to the ideas of the humanist Lorenzo Valla, and my contention is that there was no-one with whom he was more at home than Scotus. He shared his thinking on large matters and small.

The point I wish to stress is that Mair's Scotism was bound to have a direct influence on other thinkers, including, and especially, Scots. For first, Mair was, as stated above, one of the luminaries among the teachers of the University of Paris. He published what he taught in his lectures, and we know him therefore to have given lectures that had a distinctly Scotist hue. In this context the fact, just mentioned, that Mair headed a team that edited one of Scotus's major works, is especially significant, for Mair must have intended that edition as a teaching aid. He wanted his students to know about Scotus and it was, as he saw it, important that they had to hand as reliable an edition as possible.

Amongst his many students at Paris there was a large contingent of Scots, some of whom in their turn became regents and professors at the university. Others who had never studied under him were colleagues living with him at the College of Montaigu in Paris and with whom he must have discussed his philosophical and theological ideas. It has to be recalled in this context that these men were no mere career academics; all the academic questions they dealt with on a daily basis were seen by them as relating, more or less directly, to matters of life and death and the salvation of souls. Academic questions about, for example, the nature of will and intellect, and about our relations to the world in which we live, were not entertaining diversions but deeply important questions that could have a profound effect on the way articles of faith were formulated and understood. The writings of the men I am speaking of are full of a tone of high moral seriousness because they were responding in a responsible way to the sovereign importance of the issues, and so of course at every opportunity these academics would discuss with each other the problems they were working on. In many ways they lived in each others' academic pockets. This formidable contingent of Scots included Hector Boece (c.1465-1536) of Dundee who taught at Paris before returning to Scotland to become first principal of the University of Aberdeen. He was a logician and author of a fine textbook on logic. He was also a friend and admirer of Mair of whom he wrote that he was 'a profound theologian, whose writings, like brightest torches, have shed a glorious light on the Christian religion'. There were also David Cranston (c.1479-1512), priest of the Glasgow diocese, a brilliant and prolific philosopher; Gilbert Crab (c.1482-1522) of Aberdeen who published on Aristotle's *Politics* while he was still a student; Robert Galbraith (c.1483-1544) who became, in turn, professor of Roman Law at the University of Paris and Senator of the College of Justice in Edinburgh, and who was author of one of the great works of logic of the late Middle Ages; George Lokert (c.1485-1547) of Ayr, who rose to become prior of the Sorbonne, Rector of St Andrews University and dean of Glasgow; William Manderston (c.1485-1552), graduate of Glasgow University who became successively rector of the University of Paris and of the University of St Andrews. The point to be stressed is that many of this galaxy of thinkers returned to Scotland, as did Mair himself, to form the topmost stratum in the country's education system, the ones who set the tone and the standard. And all of them had come under the spell of Mair. In these circumstances the thinking of Scotus was bound to influence the thinking of the generation of intellectual leaders in Scotland as the country headed towards the Reformation. This was of course a generation that included John Knox, who is now generally recognised as having studied under Mair in St Andrews in the early 1530s, and who, in a famous phrase in his *History of the Reformation in Scotland*, referred to Mair as a man whose word was then held as 'an oracle on matters of religion'.

Some years ago I argued that though John Duns Scotus was the first truly great Scottish philosopher the origins of philosophy in Scotland cannot helpfully be dated before 1411/12 when the University of St Andrews was established; and on that basis I began my account of the tradition of Scottish philosophy with Lawrence of Lindores, the first major philosopher at St Andrews. In light of all I have been saying in this chapter I now believe that it would have been better to have included Scotus in my account of the tradition even though Scotus himself did no philosophical work in this country and had, so far as is known, no philosophical impact whatever on Scotland in his own lifetime. And this judgment has to be made largely because of the way Scotus was appropriated by subsequent generations of Scots, taken up into their thinking, so that their thinking was in crucial ways of a piece with his.

There were indeed Scottish philosophers even earlier than Scotus, men such as Richard of St Victor (Ricardus de Sancto Victore Scotus c.1123-73), prior of the abbey of St Victor in Paris, Adam Scot, abbot of Dryburgh, and Michael Scot (d.1236), whose work made a big impact in their own day, and whose writings have survived to the present. It can be argued that Richard of St Victor in particular played a significant role in the tradition of Scottish philosophy. He was a philosopher-theologian who constructed a detailed theology of the Trinity, one centring on the idea of love. He held that God is related to himself by the relation of love, that the Son and the Holy Spirit were produced by God in an act of love, and that therefore in so far as we approach the created order with an attitude of love our lives are an imitation of the divine, the highest form of living that is available to us creatures. These doctrines of the twelfth century Richard of St Victor are important in relation to the thesis of this book, because they were taken up into Franciscan theology in the thirteenth century almost as soon as the Franciscan Order was founded, and those same doctrines had an immense influence on the thinking of Richard's compatriot the Franciscan friar John Duns Scotus. Though I shall be arguing that it is appropriate to describe a significant swathe of the Scottish philosophical tradition as Scotist it should not be forgotten that the intellectual world to which Scotus was heir had received significant input from Scots. However there is no doubt that the towering figure in pre-Reformation Scottish philosophy was Scotus himself, and that he cast a shadow far beyond the Middle Ages, into the Age of Enlightenment and beyond. Much of this book will be taken up with a justification of that description of his place in Scottish culture.

More immediately I pause on the common perception that the high point of Scottish culture was the awesome event known as the Scottish Enlightenment. During a period of rather more than half a century, a few decades on either side of 1750, the contribution that Scots made to European and world culture was immense, wildly disproportionate to the country's population and level of prosperity. In philosophy, aesthetics, economics, social theory, in physics, chemistry, geology – the list is long – Scotland produced world-beaters. No-one doubts that the event was a high point of Scottish culture, but the question whether it was or was not *the* high point calls for an ample perspective; and certainly not one confined to the post-Reformation period, for we have a long history. In particular it must be emphasised that the Age of Enlightenment was not the first occasion on which Scotland was a major performer in the field of high culture. The late-medieval period was another such, when again, as we have seen, Scotland produced not simply individual high-fliers, but rather individuals in dialogue, each impelling the others to dig deeper into their souls in search of new truths. There is no suggestion in this that the circle of John Mair constituted in some way an Enlightenment before the Enlightenment. Such a suggestion has to be resisted if the term 'Enlightenment' is to retain any value as a useful classificatory tool for historians of ideas. Nevertheless there are significant similarities between the two events, separated though they are by more than two centuries. And these similarities have to be noted if we are to speak about a 'Scottish philosophy' and by this phrase refer to something other than the sum of philosophical writings produced by Scots.

For many people the phrase 'philosophy of the Scottish Enlightenment' means first and foremost, or even solely, David Hume (1711-76). But there is far more to the philosophical dimension of the Scottish Enlightenment than Hume. In definable respects indeed he wrote against the grain of the tradition rather than with it, as I shall seek to demonstrate, and some of the best Scottish philosophy was written in response to and as a refutation of Hume. I shall be emphasising the part of the Scottish philosophy of the Enlightenment that set itself up against, and as an alternative to, Hume. But it is also necessary to note that Hume's philosophical roots, which ran deep and wide, were nourished by Scottish predecessors, most notably by Francis Hutcheson (1694-1746), who was elected professor of philosophy in the University of Glasgow in 1729, and was declared professor of moral philosophy in the following year. This enormously influential man attracted the unstinting praise of his successor in the moral philosophy chair, Adam Smith (1723-90). Smith, a profound writer on ethics, spoke of 'the never to be forgotten Hutcheson', and plainly learnt a great deal from his predecessor. However, it was Hume more than anyone else who did magical things with Hutcheson's ideas. We shall look briefly at the Humean magic. Paradoxically one wonderful outcome of those magical things was the birth of a school of thought that engendered several profound works deeply hostile to Hume's system. I have in mind the Scottish school of common sense philosophy.

The leader of the school was Thomas Reid, a member, through his mother, of the formidable Gregory family, the most distinguished dynasty of the Scottish Enlightenment. After schooling in Aberdeen he began, aged twelve, the four-year arts course at Marischal College, Aberdeen, under the philosopher-theologian George Turnbull. He proceeded to the study of theology and in 1731 became a minister of the Church of Scotland. Reid was thereafter, in turn, librarian at Marischal, minister at the village of New Machar in Aberdeenshire, and regent at King's College, Aberdeen. In 1758 he helped to found the Aberdeen Philosophical Society, the 'Wise Club', which included, among other philosophers, George Campbell, Alexander Gerard and James Beattie. It was during this period that Reid developed many of the distinctive doctrines of his philosophy of common sense, and no doubt a number of the doctrines were aired in discourses on perception and on the senses which Reid delivered to the Aberdeen Philosophical Society between 1758 and 1763. In 1764, his final year in Aberdeen, he published the first of his three major works, *An Inquiry into the Human Mind on the Principles of Common Sense*, which is in part a powerful critique of Hume's philosophy of perception. The book is however also a constructive exercise aimed at replacing Hume's theory with a better one.

In 1764 Reid succeeded Adam Smith as professor of moral philosophy at the University of Glasgow. He continued to develop his philosophy of common sense, and (though retaining his chair) retired from teaching in 1780 in order to prepare his ideas for publication. His *Essays on the Intellectual Powers of Man*, which appeared in 1785, were followed three years later by *Essays on the Active Powers of the Human Mind*. His ideas continued to dominate in Aberdeen and Glasgow long after he ceased to teach in those universities, and those ideas were also taken up and developed in Edinburgh, most importantly by Dugald Stewart (1753-1828). Stewart attended Edinburgh University before going to Glasgow to study under Thomas Reid. During this latter period, while still only eighteen, he wrote an essay on dreaming, which he later incorporated into his *Elements of the Philosophy of the Human Mind*, a work very heavily influenced by Reid. Stewart duly succeeded his father in the chair of mathematics at Edinburgh, and in 1785, when Adam Ferguson, professor of moral philosophy at Edinburgh, retired from teaching, Stewart transferred to Ferguson's chair. His voice was the dominant one on behalf of common sense philosophy in Edinburgh until Sir William Hamilton (1788-1856) took on the role.

When James Ferrier, professor of moral philosophy at St Andrews, spoke of the 'Scottish philosophy' it was the philosophy of common sense that he had in mind. This Scottish philosophy, in its eighteenth-century guise, was stimulated by Hume. Reid tells us: 'I never thought of calling in question the principles commonly received with regard to the human understanding, until the *Treatise of Human Nature* was published in the year 1739.' (*Inquiry*, p.3) It was therefore Hume's *Treatise* that awoke Reid from his dogmatic slumbers, just as some decades later it was Hume also who, on Immanuel Kant's own testimony, awoke Kant from his dogmatic slumbers. And indeed in certain respects Reid and Kant look in the same direction for a way to defuse Hume's sceptical challenge, so much so that Reid came to be called the 'Scottish Kant' – perhaps a trifle unfairly since Reid was working on his common sense resolution of Humean scepticism some four decades before Kant published his own resolution in the *Critique of Pure Reason*, (though I do not intend to argue here that Kant should be called 'the German Reid'!)

The routes from medieval Scotland to the Scottish Enlightenment are complex and complexly interrelated, and fortunately they are not my business here. But as an indication of the complexities that have to be investigated it should be noted that John Mair taught a number of Spanish students while at the University of Paris. They returned to Spain and taught his philosophy there; Mair's books were compulsory reading in several Spanish universities during the sixteenth century. Among his Spanish students was Francisco Vitoria, a great jurisprudentialist and innovative writer on law and morality who quotes Mair frequently. Francisco Suarez, a successor of Vitoria and a towering figure in the field of jurisprudence and the philosophy of law, also quotes Mair frequently and always with respect. Suarez was taken up and developed by the great German jurist Samuel Pufendorf, whose work was the subject of a commentary by Gershom Carmichael, first professor of moral philosophy at the University of Glasgow, who was succeeded in his chair by the extraordinary trio, Francis Hutcheson, Adam Smith and then Thomas Reid. As well as intellectual routes that stay within Scotland, there are therefore other routes also, such as the one just delineated, less direct but none the less substantive, that have to be taken into account in the determination of links between Scottish philosophy of the pre-Reformation period and the Enlightenment. It is to John Duns Scotus, presiding genius of this nation of philosophers and the first major link in the chain of the Scottish philosophical tradition, that I now turn.

CHAPTER 3

On being free: a medieval perspective

Western philosophy from almost its earliest days has spoken of human beings in terms of a dichotomy. For we are described as thinkers looking out upon the world and trying to understand it, and we are also described as agents seeking to make changes to the world which we, as thinkers, have come to understand. This 'thinker-agent' dichotomy leads directly to another, for it is in virtue of our faculty of intellect, or understanding, that we can think and it is in virtue of our faculty of will that we can act. Scotus's account of the mind is directed largely to an investigation of these two faculties and of the relations between them, and I shall present an account of his leading doctrines in this field. But first it is necessary to emphasise a point concerning Scotus's understanding of the relation between the two faculties, for to speak of them as two is immediately to prompt a question concerning the sense in which they are two and not one. I shall begin by dealing with that question.

Scotus maintains that the mind has a unity of a particularly strong sort. There are different sorts of unity. A heap of pebbles has a unity, but it is not so strong a unity that the heap is much affected if a pebble is removed. There is still a heap there, and removal of the one pebble may make absolutely no perceptible difference either to the heap as a whole or to the other pebbles. A living thing, a tree, say, or an animal, has a different kind of unity, for in it there is a systematic relation between the various parts so that the loss of, say, a limb is bound to have effects elsewhere in the organism. Nevertheless after the loss the organism can continue to live and even flourish.

What then of the unity of the mind? There can be no unity which does not contain a multiplicity, for a unity implies the presence of things united. Something which contains no multiplicity might be one or a oneness, but lacking things united in it, it cannot be a unity. If then the mind has a unity there must be things united in it, and of course there are – its faculties, intellect, will, memory, and so on. Having therefore some kind of unity we must ask what kind, whether that of the heap of pebbles, or that of the organism; or perhaps some other comparison is more apposite.

If a person has no memory, absolutely no memory rather than merely having a poor one, then he cannot remember the immediately antecedent sentence while reading the present one, nor can he remember the beginning of this sentence while reading the end of it, nor the beginning of a word while reading the end of it. Indeed with absolutely no memory he cannot read. A person so bereft is unable to hold anything in his mind long enough to engage in any intellectual exercise whatever. The mind must be supposed therefore to have a strong kind of unity to this extent at least, that if a person's memory is annihilated then none of the other mental faculties will be able to function.

Further evidence of the unity of the mind is gleaned by consideration of the mutual dependence of intellect and will. To consider first the dependence of will on intellect, in light of Scotus's doctrine: every act of will is directed to an end, the object willed. At the time of the act of will the object does not yet exist; indeed the purpose of the act is precisely to bring the object into existence. But the object must exist in some way, at least in the agent's head, if he is to know what he is aiming at in performing the act of will. So the object can be thought of as having in succession two sorts of existence, first as a concept in the agent's mind, and then as the subsequent reality corresponding to the concept. The construction of the concept is an act of intellect. And in the absence of the concept there is no act of will. To will is to will something; something which is in the first instance conceived. To will without willing something is to will in the abstract, and an abstract act of will is not an act of will at all. Put otherwise, to will without willing something is to will nothing, and to will nothing is simply not to will. In so far as an act of will depends upon a concept of what is willed, and the concept depends upon an act of intellect to produce it, there cannot be an act of will without an antecedent act of intellect. Scotus is very clear on this matter: 'On account of that necessary relation an act of will cannot be caused by the faculty of will unless an act of understanding has already been caused by the intellect.' (Scotus in *Opera Omnia*, vol. XIII, p.212) It follows that the mind has a unity in the sense that the annihilation of the intellect implies annihilation of the will also.

I turn now to consideration of the converse of what has just been demonstrated, for it is Scotus's view that intellect depends upon will no less than does will upon intellect. The issue arises vividly in the context of his discussion of Jerome's dictum that there is sin in thought, word and deed. The immediate problem for Scotus concerns the possibility of sinning in thought. The problem arises because of the Church's teaching that every sinful act is willed. For suppose that an act of thought is sinful. In that case the act of sinful thinking must have been performed by an act of will. But, in accordance with what was argued above, we cannot will something unless we first form a concept of what we will, and hence to will a sinful thought we must first have a concept of the sinful thought. But in that case it is, so to say, already too late to will the thought. It is already there, in our mind. (*Opera Omnia*, vol. XIII, p.451) There is therefore a paradox regarding sinful thought that needs to be dealt with. It should be said that Scotus does not waver. He accepts totally Jerome's belief that there can be sinful thoughts. Scotus's problem is that of resolving the paradox.

I shall make a start on expounding his resolution by noting that, whatever the answer is, it cannot depend on the assumption that all thoughts are subject to will, for such an assumption is plainly false. There are thoughts which come into our minds unbidden; we simply find ourselves having them. But Scotus focuses on the fact that once a thought has appeared unbidden then what happens to it thereafter is indeed subject to will. He considers the parallel with visual perception. When I look out upon the visible world I have something in focus and also see other things which are closer to the periphery of my visual field. In general what is in focus is seen more distinctly and what is out of focus, though still within the visual field, is seen less distinctly. Well, as Scotus points out, the same thing happens in our thinking; for we all have frequent experience of noticing an idea out of the corner of our intellectual eye while we are thinking about some other matter. What happens next is crucial to Scotus's case. When an idea which is on the periphery of our field of intellectual vision, an idea to which we are not paying attention, draws attention to itself in virtue of some feature it possesses, we can respond to it in at least two ways. First, if the passing thought pleases us we can will to attend to it, in order to explore it and to enjoy it more deeply. Secondly, if with that first intellectual glance the passing thought displeases us, for whatever reason, we can will to give even less attention to it, or can withdraw our attention entirely, thus annihilating the idea. Scotus's example is of a lustful or lascivious thought. To delight in the thought of a morally prohibited act, and willingly to maintain the thought in existence because of the pleasure it affords, is sinful. The thought of the morally prohibited act on its first appearance in the mind is not sinful, for it arrived unbidden. But Scotus's point is that whether the thought remains in existence or not *is* subject to voluntary control, and its maintenance is therefore wilful and therefore sinful. The initial paradox is therefore resolved. A thought can indeed be willed, but not on its first appearance; what is willed is its continued presence in the mind, and therefore it is, after all, appropriate for Jerome to say that there can be sin in a thought, that is, in an act of thinking.

Scotus draws a piece of moral advice from these considerations. It is that, faced with the threat of an inner sinful act, we should will to avert our intellectual gaze. Instead of permitting our longing for an illicit object to seep corrosively into our souls, we are able and we ought to direct our attention elsewhere so that the illicit thought is annihilated. Here my purpose is not to dispute this piece of moral advice; I have taken issue with it elsewhere. I am chiefly concerned instead to underline the fact that for Scotus our intellectual life is to a very great extent, indeed almost totally, subject to voluntary control.

This is a crucial point of contact between Scotus and the Scottish common sense school. According to Scotus we have voluntary control over our mental acts no less than over the motion of our bodies. In neither case is the voluntary control total. If there were not physical movements that take place unbidden, that take place entirely by nature or by instinct, there would not be the possibility of our willing to perform acts in the physical world. Likewise though some thoughts that come into our minds come unbidden, nevertheless almost all of our mental life is willed, for we have control over the direction that our thought takes in that at any instant, and by an act of will, we can direct our intellectual gaze more precisely upon what we are in any case thinking about and we can instead direct our gaze elsewhere thereby making vanish what we had previously been attending to. If therefore there is some thought we are entertaining that is giving us a pleasure we judge undesirable, we can will the thought out of existence. If on the contrary we are entertaining an unpleasant thought, we might will to maintain that thought in existence and pursue it despite the disagreeableness of the task, because we believe that we have to think a particular problem through and that the need to work out a solution overrides considerations of disagreeableness.

It is therefore incorrect to think that the intellect has a life of its own and can get along quite nicely without the will; the truth is that intellect cannot get anywhere without the aid of will. An intellect not guided by will at every turn would be so utterly chaotic as not to be recognisably a human intellect at all. Scotus emphasises the dependence of intellect upon will no less than the dependence of will upon intellect, and his position seems unexceptionable. Intellect and will may be separable in a process of intellectual abstraction, in the sense that we can make a philosophical analysis of the two and say things about either that cannot truly be said about the other, but the two cannot be separated in existence.

Scotus's point is that there are not two distinct realities here, intellect and will; there is only one reality, the mind which engages in different kinds of act - it thinks and it wills. When it thinks it takes on the form of a thinker and when it wills it takes on the form of a willer. Earlier I asked about the strength of unity of the mind, and Scotus's response is now clear. The unity could hardly be stronger. Intellect and will, the two great faculties of mind, are different from each other only in being different forms that the mind takes when engaged in its different kinds of act. In reality therefore, intellect and will are not two but one. Or rather they are two forms of the one thing, mind. At this point I am dealing with matters that lie at the heart of what I believe to be the Scottish philosophy, and so should like to pursue further the question of the relation between intellect and will. It is a remarkable fact that the deeper into Scotus we go the more doctrines we encounter that in due course reappear in the common sense school. Let us then interrogate will.

If intellect and will are in reality the same thing, the mind that thinks and wills, does it follow that will cannot act independently of intellect? And if it cannot does it follow that will cannot perform any act that is not sanctioned by intellect? This is a critically important question for those who believe in the freedom of the will in a tough sense of the term 'freedom'. If the will cannot perform any act other than the acts dictated by intellect then the doctrine of determinism is correct. True it is intellectual determinism, determination by the intellect, but intellectual determinism is a form of determinism. However, as we shall see, the Scottish philosophical tradition is strongly on the side of the opposite doctrine, libertarianism. According to this tradition the will is free to such an extent that it is free even (or perhaps especially) in relation to the dictates of the intellect.

There is much talk these days of biological imperatives but the concept of a biological imperative, though not the terminology, has been around for a long time, as witness discussions by for example the seventeenth century philosopher Thomas Hobbes concerning the human organism's demand for its own survival, a natural demand that cannot be silenced even if we choose to act against it. Scotus knew the philosophical significance of these natural or biological imperatives. By nature we demand not only our continued existence but also nourishment, warmth, sleep, and so on. These are things that contribute to our perfection, the perfection of the biological organism, a perfection constituted by the organism's flourishing or well-functioning. The natural principle in us, in virtue of which we are naturally directed towards our own natural perfection, is in a sense a principle of passivity. For if we ever give our nature as long a leash as it wants and let it follow through the tendencies here at issue, then we are living according to nature's laws; we are responding passively to nature as it is articulated in us. Scotus allows that in one sense this inner natural principle can be called 'will'. It might be said therefore that by nature we will our survival, nourishment, warmth, sleep, and so on. But Scotus is clear that this natural principle is not 'will' properly understood, because the will, the real will, is not in any way a principle of passivity. What then is the real will?

The answer depends upon a recognition that in us humans nature does not simply have its way. The voice, sometimes shrill, of our biological nature cannot be silenced, but that does not imply that we always obey its directives. And even when we do obey its directives that is not because we have to. Even if we allow nature to take its course and let it follow through a given tendency, well, it is we who allow it to do so. I spoke above about giving our nature as long a leash as it wants, but it has to be noted that it is we who give it this long leash. We always have an alternative, which is to say 'no' to nature. That we can will contrarily to nature is demonstrated most dramatically by the fact that though the most insistent biological imperative demands that we do whatever needs to be done to keep the organism alive, we humans can will to perform an act which we know will lead to our death. The faculty of will which is able to will against our biological nature cannot be the same faculty which naturally wills obedience to those same biological imperatives. Scotus called the latter type of will a 'natural will', though adding the caution that it is not really a will at all. The other kind of will, the real will, he described as free.

A distinction is commonly made between freedom *from* something, and freedom *to do* something. These are respectively negative and positive characterisations of freedom. Scotus had both characterisations in mind. As regards the negative characterisation of freedom of the will, we are free from nature for nature does not determine will to act. This point which seems simple, so much so that its significance can be overlooked, is perhaps the single most amazing thing about us humans. Nature as a whole presents itself to us as a system of awesome, and perhaps infinite power. We are otherwise. As far as our power is concerned, as compared with nature we have so little power that it seems that to have less is to have none at all. What are we in a world of black holes and exploding supernovae? To speak about our power in the context of such great events of the cosmos seems almost an abuse of language. Yet we are not overpowered by nature. I am now typing a sentence. This is not nature's doing but mine. If my acts were determined by gravity, electromagnetism and the weak and strong nuclear forces, and by other features of the cosmos, none of this book would have been written. Nature, left to its own devices, would not type this sentence in a billion years, nor any of the other sentences in this book, and even less would it type all of them and in the order in which they appear here. But the typing of this book has not been left to nature's devices; it has been left to mine. And I have willed to do what nature would never have done, namely, type the book. When I will to perform a given act and then, as happens often enough, do what I will to do, I have squared up to nature and won. This is not a case of nature working through me to secure its own ends, but instead a case of me using nature to secure my own ends, ends which cannot be ascribed to nature.

But if nature is infinite in its power and I, by an act of will, can square up to nature and win, then my power also must be infinite. In such acts it is not I that am overpowered – nature is. Earlier I wondered whether, given the awesome power of nature, it is not an abuse of language to ascribe power to humans, so near to nothing is our power as compared with nature's. We now see, following Scotus's lead, that our power is no less awesome than nature's, and indeed it may be thought that, considering our speck-like size in the cosmos and the fleetingness of our being, our power is all the more remarkable. We shall see that the common sense philosophers of the eighteenth century took this argument of Scotus's a stage further, and argued that on the contrary we humans, having intellect and will, really do have power, and it is of such a nature, that it is hardly appropriate to speak of dead matter as having any. The position might seem counter-intuitive but it is supported by argumentation which is persuasive. I stress this position, which is strongly libertarian, because it is central to Scottish philosophy as I conceive it.

The emphasis so far has been on the negative aspect of the freedom of will, its freedom from nature. The positive aspect also can be expounded by contrast with nature. The free will is free to do what things in nature are not free to do. Whatever it is that a natural thing does in the circumstances in which it acts, it could not in those very same circumstances have done otherwise. A fire heats the kettle of water, and in those very same circumstances it could not freeze the water, nor do anything else to the water other than heat it. It might be said that the sun blackens some things and at the same time it bleaches others; it hardens mud and at the same time it melts ice, and so on. But the sun cannot do otherwise than it does do in those very same circumstances. What it does there and then to the mud it cannot not do. Likewise it can have only that effect on the ice that in fact it does have there and then. Thus nature is always constrained to a single effect.

But we are not like that. Whatever we do we could, in those very same circumstances, have done otherwise. In this sense we are not constrained to a single effect, instead we are open to contraries. This is not of course to say that we can produce contrary effects simultaneously; it is to say that in the circumstances in which we produce a given effect we could have produced a contrary one. The power to produce either of contraries in the same circumstances is termed a 'rational power' by Scotus, and the only power he knows that answers to this description is the will. There is a view that we are always constrained to will what we believe to be good, or to be the best in the circumstances. And if we are constrained to will what we believe to be good, our will is not free. But Scotus, ever the realist, rejects the first premiss of this argument, the claim that we are so constrained. Even if we cannot will to perform an act that we believe to be evil, we might yet resist the attractions of what we believe to be good. We always have the alternative of willing to do nothing rather than something, and in that sense we are indeed free because we are open to contraries. Even if we have the prospect of performing an act which will bring us happiness we are free to turn our back on it. That people, even we ourselves, do sometimes behave in this manner, is a matter of experience.

In light of this positive concept of freedom of the will, I should like to turn to the question of the relation between dictates of the intellect and acts of will. As has already been observed, an act of will always has an object, something to which it is directed, and since this object is presented to will in the form of a practical concept, a plan of action, it must have been produced by the intellect. The will is, however, always open to contraries, from which it follows that the fact that will receives a proposal by intellect does not imply that will must say 'yes' to it. Intellect proposes but will disposes, and will might dispose against the best judgment of intellect. It cannot however fail to hear the voice of intellect. Since intellect and will are really identical, both being the same as the mind which thinks and wills, will cannot act as if intellect has not spoken. But that it has to listen does not imply that it has to obey.

There are degrees of influence here. Scotus uses the phrase 'pondus et inclinatio', that is, intellect carries weight with the will and inclines it. This phrase does not imply determination of the will by intellect. But what of the case where intellect proposes a line of action that is so reasonable that to reject the proposal would be mad? In that case we will no doubt do as proposed, but that does not imply that we could not do otherwise. In that very circumstance we could do otherwise – it is simply that we would be mad to do so. That it would be crazy for us to actualise a given possibility, is no doubt our reason for not actualising it. But that does not mean that we *could not* actualise it, just that we *will not*. And of course we *might* actualise it, for sadly human beings do sometimes do mad things, even while knowing them to be mad. Anyone can do something crazy, even if, being reasonable beings, we *usually* act in a reasonable way.

It might be wondered why will is so respectful of intellect. The proposals of intellect are reasonable – that is intellect's job. But if will is not itself intellect, then how can will recognise the reasonableness of intellect's proposals? Is it not only by the intellect that we recognise the reasonableness of anything? The answer is that, at least according to Scotus, will *is* intellect. It is the one power, mind, which thinks and wills, and the mind knows when it is being reasonable. In that sense will, as being what the mind is when the mind wills, also recognises the reasonableness of intellect's proposals. It is the real identity of intellect and will that prevents will, despite its freedom, from acting in a random manner, just as it is the fact that intellect and will are distinct from each other, at least, in being distinct forms that mind takes, that allows will the distance it needs from intellect to be able to reject intellect's proposals.

Earlier I focused upon a contrast between will and everything in nature, on the basis of a distinction between something that is open to contraries and something that is constrained to a single effect. Natural things are constrained to a single effect. Scotus includes intellect among natural things. The intellect is not open to contraries, because relying on its own resources it cannot give assent to the premisses of an argument and also give assent to the validity of the argument and yet withhold assent from the conclusion. It is constrained to assent to the conclusion. If will were in play, then a different story might be told. For example it could be said that seeing, as it were, out of the corner of its intellectual eye, the conclusion to which an argument is heading and finding the conclusion disagreeable, the mind might will to switch its attention from the argument, so that the conclusion is not after all reached, at least not reached with the definitiveness and clarity that would have been achieved if the will had seen to it that the argument remained in clear focus right to the end. Intellect by itself cannot behave like that. To be open to contraries is, in a sense yet to be explored, a superior power to the power possessed by something that is constrained to a single effect. For this reason it is not surprising to find Scotus asserting that will has primacy in relation to intellect. This last doctrine is one of great philosophical interest, and I should like to end this chapter by offering an elucidation of Scotus's position.

Since Scotus thinks that intellect and will are really identical with each other, for both are really identical with the mind, one might wonder how, of these two things which are really identical with each other, one can have primacy in relation to the other. But it is necessary to deploy Scotus's doctrine that while in one sense they are really identical, they are nevertheless distinct from each other in the sense that the mind takes different forms when it takes the form of a thinker and a willer. Let us say, then, that intellect and will, though really identical, are formally distinct. I mention in passing that there are indications of the doctrine of the primacy of the will in the philosophy of Thomas Reid also, but here I am concerned with Scotus, a

Franciscan friar, and must therefore acknowledge that while his doctrine is philosophical it also has a theological dimension.

While Franciscans hold that there can be no love without knowledge, for love implies knowledge of the beloved, they hold also that love is superior to knowledge, and most especially love of God is superior to knowledge of him. Consequently if we had a choice (which in truth we cannot have) between loving God without knowing him and knowing God without loving him, it would be better if we chose the former alternative. Since love is located in the will and knowledge in the intellect, it follows that the will, as capable of the superior act, is the superior faculty. Scotus endorses this position. But it is not problem free. In particular it implies that love is subject to voluntary control – indeed that is what it means to say that love is located in the will – and this position is sufficiently questionable to call for defence. It can be defended effectively, as I shall try to show.

Like all other emotions, love is directed to an object. Love is love of X, just as affection is affection for X, fear is fear of X, and so on. Just as a thought can come into our heads unbidden but once there its maintenance is due to an act of will for we can always avert our intellectual gaze, so also an emotion can befall us unbidden but, once in place, its maintenance is due to an act of will in the sense that whether we continue to focus attention on the object of the emotion is subject to voluntary control. If we will to re-focus our attention so that the object of the emotion is no longer in sight (visual or intellectual) then the emotion subsides, for it is maintained in existence by the object. There is no suggestion in this that it is always easy to re-focus attention in this way. It is granted that it may require a great, even heroic effort of will. But the issue here is not whether redirection of attention is easy or difficult but whether it is possible. Scotus thinks it is possible. If we judge that a love which has come upon us is directed to an inappropriate or even illicit object, then we do not need to regard ourselves as stuck in an inappropriate or illicit relation with the object of our love. We can always do something about it, namely whatever needs to be done in order to direct our attention away from that object. To be convinced that nothing can be done is to be self-deceived. In the same way an emotion that is present can be strengthened or intensified by the direction of attention more precisely upon certain features of the object of the emotion. Love can be strengthened by a willing attention upon the most lovable qualities of the object and a willing restraint in our attention to the less lovable, or unlovable qualities. And to work on our emotions in this way is in many ways a desirable thing. It is to give them as rational a structure as we can manage, and the formation of our lives under rational principles is always a good thing. Giving our love as rational a structure as we can manage is, therefore, desirable. But if all the things about which I am now writing are part of our lives, and can be made more so by an act of will then, as one small element in this picture, love is, as the Franciscans believe, located in the will. However strange the doctrine may seem at first blush, there is a powerful argument for it.

No doubt Scotus was also swayed by the further consideration that we are commanded to love the Lord with all our heart and soul and mind. God would not command us to perform an act which is not subject to our voluntary control, and hence it must be possible for us to will to love God. Hence, on the basis of the Biblical proof text, it follows that love is located in the will. This is not however a philosophical argument, but a theological one, though, as has already been demonstrated, a good deal of philosophy lies immediately behind it.

Granted therefore that love is located in the will, and granted the theological premiss that love of God is a superior act to knowledge of him, the doctrine of primacy of the will seems well founded. Yet the doctrine evidently fails to respect the point that will cannot move an inch without the cooperation of intellect. Will wills something, and the something, prior to its realisation in the world, exists in the mind as a concept produced by the intellect. Hence the will is dependent upon the intellect. Will needs intellect. But intellect does not need will, and consequently intellect surely has primacy in relation to will.

Scotus notes this argument, but rejects it for, as already noted, he holds that while it is true that will depends on intellect it is no less true that intellect depends on will. It is not necessary to rehearse the arguments again. We need only note that if a cause has primacy in relation to the effect not only does intellect have primacy in relation to will but also will has primacy in relation to intellect. This matter can be resolved by recognising that there are many different kinds of cause, amongst which are instrumental cause and final cause. They both figure in a relation to which Scotus draws our attention, that of means to an end. (*Opera Omnia*, vol. XXI, p.115) The end depends upon the means. If there are no means by which we can reach a given end then we will not reach it. So the end depends for its realisation upon the means. But the means are adopted for the sake of the end. In that sense, the end is the final cause of the means. Hence if we did not have an end that required the adoption of those means, the means would not be adopted. The act productive of the end would not exist. Again the dependence relation is plain, but this time it proceeds in the opposite direction: the means depend upon the end for their existence.

However, there is one respect, and that the most important, in which, as regards means and end, the dependency is not mutual. The means are adopted for the sake of the end, and not vice versa. We judge some act in our power to have such a value that it is proper that we seek to bring that value into the world by performing the act. In order to perform the act we need to adopt means. The means we choose thereby acquire a value. From being valueless they acquire instrumental value, that is, they acquire the kind of value that an instrument has *qua* instrument in relation to the end that we have adopted. When Scotus speak of primacy it is the primacy of value that he has in mind.

I think that these considerations concerning the means-end relation are to the fore in Scotus's mind when he discusses the comparative worth of the acts of knowing God and loving him. It is not possible to love God except through knowing him. But the knowledge is a route to love. The love has sovereign value, but what value has the knowledge if it does not lead to love? I think that for Scotus, the situation is somewhat as with a person who smells the perfume of a rose but who is so constituted as to derive absolutely no pleasure from this, or a person who can see Botticelli's 'Venus' perfectly well but takes no delight in it, or is even bored by it. The heavenly perfume and the Botticelli are wasted on such people. They are, we imagine, no better off for having the olfactory or visual experience. The knowledge they gain is deprived of value by the failure to enter the aesthetic dimension. I believe it to have been Scotus's view that knowledge of God without love of him is no less a failure, a form of deprivation. What it is deprived of is love, an act located in the will.

With these latter thoughts I have strayed into the field of theology, especially the theology associated with St Francis. It cannot come as a surprise if the Church of Scotland minister Thomas Reid is not prepared to go all the way with Scotus on these matters – though I find nothing in the thoughts that need prove an obstacle, whether doctrinal or otherwise, to their adoption, even enthusiastic adoption, by a minister of the Kirk. But as regards all the preceding material concerning free will and its relation to the intellect, Thomas Reid is in almost total agreement with Scotus. I shall be spelling out the agreement in detail in Chapter Eight, as support for my claim that we are looking here at the kernel of the Scottish philosophy. I imagine it to be pure coincidence that Scotus was exploring the power of the human will and the concept of freedom while a war of independence was being waged in Scotland but, if not a coincidence, it provides a happy example of the unity of theory and practice.

CHAPTER 4

Looking out upon the world

Scotus's espousal of what almost all of us believe about the will, that it is free in a sense that implies a rejection of determinism, is matched by his espousal of what almost all of us believe about the senses, namely that they are reliable as a means of delivering up information about what is in the world. In short, he rejects scepticism about the external world just as he rejects scepticism about our freedom. We shall see in due course that the first of these two forms of scepticism, no less than the second, was also in the sights of the members of the eighteenth century school of Scottish common sense philosophy. We have to remember that philosophers took a stand against scepticism because others espoused scepticism. The thesis of this book is that the Scottish philosophical tradition is overwhelmingly against the sceptics, and this despite the fact that one of the three greatest of Scottish philosophers, David Hume, propounded a philosophy that he himself described (as the other two also would have done) as sceptical.

Why should we be sceptical about our power to know what is really out there? For the sake of developing my Scottish theme, I shall focus upon a line of argument that starts from the fact that there has to be some transaction between perceiver and thing perceived if an act of perception is to take place. Let us consider visual perception. How is the distance between perceiver and object overcome? The philosophers of the Middle Ages appropriated an idea, more than a millennium old even then, that there radiate from objects likenesses or similitudes of those objects, some of which strike appropriately placed sensory receptors and the likenesses duly find their way into the perceiver's mind and inform it. The medieval thinkers had a great deal to say about the physics and physiology of this transaction, but their scientific account is now hopelessly antiquated and need not detain us. There is however a modern scientific account that is offered in its place, and that gives rise to very similar philosophical problems.

These problems led to major advances in Scottish thinking in the Middle Ages and during the Scottish Enlightenment. Chief amongst the problems is the apparent implication that our knowledge of things in the outside world is indirect, mediated by the radiating similitudes (commonly known as species) or by their modern equivalent, photons perhaps (and perhaps other things also). These are things through which we come to know the objects. But if we know external objects only through these intermediaries, is it then possible that we do not really know the external objects, and that the intermediaries are not so much facilitators of perception of external objects as obstacles to it? For what we really know are the intermediaries rather than the objects from which they radiate.

A plausible way in which to understand the account of perception here under discussion is to think of the radiating intermediaries as coming to exist in the mind in the form of mental images of the objects which they represent. Since the images are similitudes of the external objects that cause them, then by a kind of inference we know that the originals exist, for if the effect (the image) exists then so also does the cause (the external object), and we also know what the originals look like – they look like the images (or perhaps I should say that they are what the images look like). But Scotus does not approve of any of this. The crucial weakness is that the images tell us nothing about whether what they are images of do or do not exist. Put otherwise, the images are indifferent to existence. Let us suppose that we observe an external object, one in the material world, and that some time later we imagine the object, that is, we form a mental image of it. Our cognition (or 'notion') of the image is not of such a nature as to yield knowledge of whether the object in external reality still exists. Yet we look out upon the world of external reality and judge continually of the existence of real things, of substances and their qualities. There must therefore be more than one kind of cognition (or notion), first, the kind by which we cognise mental images but not in such a way as to judge of the existence of things, and secondly an utterly different kind of cognition by which we cognise external things *as existing* – utterly different because the first kind of cognition (or notion) is indifferent to existence whereas the second kind is *of* existence. In order to account for our knowledge of the external world, therefore, Scotus posits a kind of cognition which yields immediate or direct knowledge of the existence of external things. He calls it intuition or intuitive cognition, and contrasts it with abstractive cognition, the kind that abstracts from, or is indifferent to existence. It might be said that there is no such thing as intuitive cognition, but Scotus's brief reply would be that if there is not then we do not have knowledge of the existence of an external reality.

For the sake of clarification a crucial distinction has to be made here between *that which* is perceived and *that by which* it is perceived. Let us return to our starting point, the fact that in the case of visual perception there is a distance to be overcome and that the overcoming of it implies the presence of intermediaries. That there are intermediaries does not mean that we have to be aware of them. Scotus's view is that partly through the work of the intermediaries we have a perceptual cognition (or a notion) of the object, but it is not through *awareness* of the intermediaries that we are aware of the object. That is, the cognition of the object is mediated by the similitudes but not by *cognition* of them. And in so far as cognition of the object is not mediated by cognition of something else, the cognition of the object is unmediated. That is, it is intuitive. We have, therefore, a direct route to the existence of external reality, direct in the sense that it is not by knowing something else that we know real objects outside the mind. Hence we are not confined to knowledge of things, images, in our own heads.

It is Scotus's view that we can have certainty regarding the existence of external objects, a certainty that is based upon the immediacy of the cognition. Such certainty is impossible in the case of abstractive cognition. If I imagine something that I had seen previously, and therefore am having an abstractive cognition of it, then even if the imaginative act gives rise to a judgment of the past existence of the thing presently imagined it cannot give rise to a judgment, made with certainty, concerning the present existence of the thing. For between the past intuitive cognition and the present abstractive one the thing might, for all I know, have ceased to exist. The certainty of what presently exists arises by purely natural means and is not subject to voluntary control. I open my eyes and see a keyboard. In that moment I am as certain of the existence of the keyboard as I am of my own existence, and I can do absolutely nothing about it. The certainty is irresistible. In that moment I am, as it were, confronted by the brute fact of my own certainty. Subsequently I can, in ways indicated in the previous chapter, set about doing things that might undermine that certainty, but in the first moment of opening my eyes it is too soon to have undermined what nature has imposed upon me, an existential certainty – certainty, that is, of a present existence.

I might learn of the present existence of an object in external reality because someone tells me that he is looking at it and, because I trust him, I am certain that the object now exists. Does that mean that, through trusting another's word, I can have the sort of existential certainty of a presently existing object that I have when I am myself in direct perceptual contact with it? The brief answer is 'no', for trust always involves an act of will. Trust can only be given freely. In this case therefore my certainty concerning the present existence of the object is not like the certainty that I have when, without my will playing a part, I open my eyes and in that instant am certain of the present existence of what I see.

Intuitive cognition gives rise to certainty by purely natural means; that is, natural causation alone is involved. But certainty due in part to an act of will is due in part to free causation. Hence such certainty does not arise from intuitive cognition. The only other sort of cognition is abstractive, and hence where our certainty about the present existence of an external object arises because we are taking someone's word for it, this implies that we have only an abstractive cognition of the object despite the fact that the cognition shares with an intuitive cognition of the object the associated existential certainty of a present object.

Scotus's doctrine of intuitive cognition gives no hint of scepticism concerning presently existing external objects. On the contrary the doctrine is evidently conceived by him as a response to what he clearly regards as a sceptical implication in the doctrine of perceptual cognition that he inherited. On the matter of the existence of an external reality Scotus was as realist as anyone could be. Not for him philosophies that teach that the reality in which, and with which, we live is somehow a product of our own imaginative or intellectual activity.

I should add, as a historical footnote to this discussion, that though Scotus was not the first philosopher to deploy the terminology of 'intuitive cognition (or notion)', he developed the concept into something peculiarly his own, and during the remainder of the Middle Ages there was virtual unanimity among philosophers that the concept was Scotus's invention. It turned out to be an immensely rich concept, full of potential for development in a host of directions. It soon came under attack, for example by Scotus's fellow Franciscan William Ockham; equally there were those who came to its defence. I shall turn now to a discussion of intuitive and abstractive cognitions (or notions), taking as my guides Scotus's compatriots John Mair, George Lokert and other members of Mair's circle.

Some philosophical questions are perennial, and the question concerning the relation between on the one hand our concepts or notions of external things and on the other hand the things themselves is one such. It occupied Scotus and two and half centuries later it occupied Mair and his colleagues. In the intervening period the discussion had been taken forward, but each position established was no more than a holding operation. It was agreed that there has to be some sort of physical transaction between knower and known if we are to have sensory perception of the world, but the nature of the transaction was a matter for dispute, as also was the nature of the mental acts involved. Although Scotus's talk about intuitive cognitions or notions and abstractive ones became common currency among philosophers and theologians and although the distinction itself was in a sense accepted, substantive questions remained about the appropriate way to formulate it, partly because Scotus was silent or obscure on many questions relating to intuitive notions, for example on the question of the precise nature of the similitudes or 'species' that radiate from an external object and produce intuitive notions. Are these species physical and, if so, are they physical in the way in which the object itself is physical or in the sense in which the qualities of the object, such as its shape or its colour are physical? Do the species have depth, or just length and breadth (assuming that they have length and breadth)? Do they, crudely stated, have a front and a back, or just a front? If they are physical, how do they manage not to obstruct our perception of the objects from which they radiate? Or perhaps they are not physical, but if not then what kind of thing are they? These are detailed questions to which Scotus does not give a reply, or at least does not give a consistent reply. Nevertheless his theory of intuitive and abstractive notions set the agenda for many including, as just noted, John Mair and his friends.

The nature of similitudes or species was an acknowledged problem and one never fully resolved, except so far as one considers the total rejection of their existence a resolution. But one has to be clear about what was considered to be at stake. One answer is that the medieval philosophers were suspicious of the concept of action at a distance, if acceptance of that doctrine committed them to the claim that of two mutually distant objects, A and B, A can cause a change in B without their being between them anything that contributes to the effect that A has on B. For example, how can I see an object a mile away, and yet there be nothing occurring or moving between me and the object that makes the perception possible?

George Lokert of Ayr discusses two cases of action at a distance, one being the magnet that attracts a distant piece of iron, and the other the torpedo fish that causes trembling in the hand of the fisherman holding the net though it does not cause trembling in the net itself. As regards the magnet's power it might be responded that the magnet has an effect (even if unperceived) on the intervening air, and without that effect it could not attract the iron – much as it might be said (and often was) that the fire heats the distant stone and does it by heating the intervening air, and it is the air immediately surrounding the stone that heats the stone. And as regards the power of the torpedo fish, it can be said, as Lokert says, that the fish does perhaps have an effect on the net, though not the effect of making the net tremble, and without this effect on the net the hand holding the net would not be affected in the way it is. The implication of these comments is that the fact that we cannot see what is taking place between two mutually distant objects does not imply that there is nothing there. It just means that we cannot see what there is. This doctrine is applied by Lokert to the species intermediate between object and perceiver. He is convinced that there is no such thing as action at a distance, and concludes that since we do see distant things there must be something between the distant object and ourselves that explains the effectiveness of the distant object in producing a perception. Species are therefore invoked (or invented) by philosophers to explain the apparent action at a distance. Though we cannot see species, Lokert does not conclude that they do not exist; he simply concludes that, as he puts it: 'they are not perceptible by sense'. (*Scriptum* sig.c 5 *recto*). Let us say therefore that species have the status of explanatory concepts; they enable us to explain the otherwise inexplicable. That we do not see them is no doubt something of a drawback, from the point of view of convincing the doubtful of their existence; but whether we see them or not, something answering to their description must be there, for if they were not, we could never perceive distant things.

Lokert believes both that we do not see species radiating from the external object and also that we see the object. Species are not an obstacle to seeing the object for they are invisible; on the contrary they are facilitators for they enable us to overcome the distance between ourselves as perceivers and the distant object. Let us now consider the two main ways in which we can relate cognitively to the external object, that is, by having an intuitive cognition or notion of it, and having an abstractive one. No member of Mair's circle doubted that we have intuitive cognitions or notions, these being mental acts of such a nature as to give rise, naturally and irresistibly, to a judgment about the existence of things and of their qualities. It is the fact that we have such perceptual intuitions that led to the invention of species or similitudes in the intervening space. Someone might then try to argue that if it is the species that we know directly, then perhaps we do not really know the external object at all, and have a right to be sceptical about whether there is such a thing. But none of our pre-Reformation Scots would have accepted that line of argument, and indeed the sceptical line is logically odd. For it grants first that our direct knowledge of external objects gives rise to the invention of the concept of an intermediary species, and then it uses the existence of the intermediary species as grounds for scepticism about the existence of the external object, the very object but for which we would not have thought of inventing the concept of the species. This is a crazy logic. The obvious thing to say in response to it is that if we are not entitled to claim direct knowledge of external objects, then the only reason we have for invoking (or inventing) species carries no weight.

Mair quite often justifies a move with phrases such as *hoc docet experientia* – experience teaches this. One of the things he is quite clear about is that experience teaches us that sensory perception involves several partial causes, one of which is the perceived external object, the second of which is whatever it is, the so-called 'species', by which the distant object eventually produces a modification in our sensory receptors, and the third of which is an act of the intellect. The act in question is an act of judgment by which we judge that there exists an external object present to us, and judge it also to have such and such qualities. Often will is also involved in our acts of judgment. As indicated earlier, whenever we take something on trust, decide to take someone's word for it, commit ourselves to a position when we are free to reject it, then there is an act of will. And a great deal of what we believe, including everything that we believe on the authority of another, is believed by an act of will. That is, the judgment that a given proposition is true is an effect of will and not just of nature.

But in the case we are considering here, the intuitive cognition or notion of an external reality, will plays no part. The mental act is directed to, and terminates at, the external object, and the perceiver can do absolutely nothing about assenting to the judgment that the object exists. He can refuse to open his eyes, of course, but he cannot look at the object without judging irresistibly that the object is present to him. This point prompts a question, duly raised by Mair, concerning what it is to which an act of abstractive cognition is directed. His answer is based upon experience. The distinction between the two types of cognition or notion, the intuitive and the abstractive, is roughly the difference between on the one hand perceiving something and on the other hand remembering it. And it is obvious that in this sort of case the abstractive cognition terminates at the external object just as does, and just as much as does, the intuitive cognition. The difference between the two types of cognition is therefore not a difference regarding their object; it is instead a difference regarding the judgment that we naturally and irresistibly make concerning the external existence of the object. If all our cognitions were abstractive there would be ample room for scepticism about the existence of an external world – assuming of course that if all our cognitions were abstractive we could even form the concept of an external world. But we do not have room for being sceptical on this matter, or rather, nature does not allow us room for such scepticism.

Nevertheless Mair allows (as how could he not?) that it is possible to form an abstractive cognition or notion of something that we have not previously perceived. He considers the notion he has of an elephant and tells us how he came by it: 'I am told that an elephant is a white animal with a large curved nose and with a castle on its back. Previously I have seen noses and white horses and castles. And I form notions of these things that I have sensed elsewhere ... And the intellect can unite these simple notions.' (*In 1 Sent.* 34 *recto*) It is in this context that Mair mentions that he has never seen St Andrews (this was in 1510), but has an abstractive notion of it because someone has told him about 'the castle, the North Sea, the college, and the other things'. The philosophical point of this fragment of autobiography is that on the basis of prior experience we can form an abstractive notion of something of which we have never had an intuitive notion. Nevertheless if we are to form an abstractive notion in this way, there are certain intuitive notions that we must previously have had. An abstractive notion of St Andrews, or of an elephant, is complex or composite, and though it is not necessary for us to have had a unitary intuitive notion of the complex object of the abstractive notion, it is necessary for us to have had intuitive notions corresponding to the parts of the object of the abstractive notion. This is a tough-minded empiricism with no sceptical tendencies.

The doctrine that intuitive notions yield truth was common to the members of Mair's circle. Lokert, for example, affirms: 'An intuitive notion is one through which a contingent truth about the notion's object can be known, for example, the truth that the object is pale or seated, distant or near, or that the object exists or does not exist. An abstractive notion is the opposite. Through it no contingent truth about its object can be known.' (*Scriptum* sig.c 7 *recto*) This linkage of intuition and truth is a potential source of trouble to these philosophers. For the standard case of having an intuitive cognition or notion is the case of a person who opens his eyes and sees whatever it is that is right in front of him, or who puts his hand on a table top and feels the firmness and smoothness of the table. Of course we are certain of the truth of the perceptual judgment that we promptly make, but our philosophers were aware that we sometimes make mistakes in our perceptual judgments. Mair imagines the case of somebody whirling a firebrand round his head and observers seeing what they judge to be an unbroken circle of fire, and the case of a raindrop falling off an eave and observers seeing what, because of the velocity of the raindrop, they judge to be a continuous stream of water.

In response to the fact of such cases Mair comments: 'Erroneous judgments are produced in many ways, but rarely in the intellect.' (*In 1 Sent*. 34 *verso*) He has in mind the fact that although we might be deceived frequently if we relied solely upon the evidence of a single sense, our perceptual judgments are sometimes mutually inconsistent; and intellect, which does not like inconsistencies, for its first law is 'Be ye consistent', proceeds to determine which of the mutually inconsistent judgments should be rejected. We might judge something to be at a distance because it is small, and we then discover that it is in reach. Or something might look like an apple, but when we lift it up it is evident from the weight that it is stone or metal painted to resemble an apple. And as Mair points out, as the person moves the firebrand more slowly the appearance of an unbroken circle of flame ceases, and we realise that our earlier judgment was erroneous.

The significance of these examples is that they point to the fact that we do not hesitate to use a perceptual judgment based on one perceptual act to check a judgment made on the basis of a previous perceptual act. The fact therefore that a perceptual judgment can be erroneous is not regarded as sanctioning a general scepticism about the reliability of our senses to deliver up the truth. It is, after all, only because we regard our senses as in general reliable that it is appropriate to use our senses to corroborate, or to disconfirm an earlier judgment based upon a given perceptual act. This doctrine duly reappears in detail in the writings of Thomas Reid. The doctrine is common sense, or 'realist' as it would have been described in the Middle Ages.

CHAPTER 5

The Will to Believe

The doctrine of the unity of mind, maintained by Scotus, was also maintained by John Mair and his circle. The unity in question is of such a nature as to rule out a crudely physical model of mind. True, mind has several faculties which might be thought of as the parts out of which it is constructed. But this idiom, 'the parts out of which mind is constructed', misleads so far as it suggests that faculties can exist independently of each other, and can be brought together to form a mind somewhat as a wall is constructed out of bricks. The idiom also suggests that one part of mind can be removed while leaving the rest intact. In Chapter Three we noted Scotus's demonstration that the various faculties, in particular, intellect and will, have to be present if the mind is to function in a recognisably human way. We recall that for Scotus intellect and will are in reality the same; they are the mind so far as it is engaged in different sorts of act, thinking and willing. Furthermore, will is not switched off when we think, neither is intellect switched off when we will. Acts of will and of intellect are generally simultaneous. Indeed it is perhaps better to remind ourselves of the fact that the distinction between acts of will and acts of intellect can indeed be made as an exercise in philosophical analysis, but that the philosophically distinct things cannot be separated in reality. That is to say, there are mental acts in which can be distinguished intellectual and volitional components, where the volitional component depends for its existence on the intellectual component and vice versa. There is therefore reason to hold that our mental acts have a unity no less tight-bound than has the mind whose acts they are. In this chapter I should like to discuss a kind of mental act in which the unitary exercise of intellect and will is particularly conspicuous. The act in question is the 'assent of faith' – saying 'yes' as an act of faith.

In the discussion of sensory perception in Chapter Four we attended to a particular kind of assent. We open our eyes and see an object before us, and assent immediately to a proposition concerning both the existence of the object and also its qualities. It is a red-backed book that I am looking at and in that moment I cannot doubt its existence. In that moment my will is not engaged. Thereafter it is engaged, for I do not have to continue to attend to the book. I can instead look at something else and I can instead close my eyes. It is true that sometimes I am 'riveted' by what I am looking at, but this is not to imply that in the face of the attention-holding qualities of the object of my gaze I have lost my freedom of will. It implies only that it would take an effort of will to avert my gaze. Which is another way of saying that I am free to look elsewhere. But in the first moment of looking and seeing what I see, I assent by nature to a proposition concerning the existence of the thing. Such assent was termed 'evident assent'. It is naturally caused and is given unhesitatingly.

Not all assent is of that nature, nor even all assent arising from a perceptual act. We see something but are not quite sure whether it is a bird or a plane (or a man?). But we think that it is a plane, and so say 'yes' to the proposition. The 'yes' however is said hesitantly. There is evidence, the slightly blurred evidence of our own eyes, but it is not the same quality of evidence as the evidence I have if in clear daylight I stare at a book that is just twelve inches away from me. Likewise, if someone I do not know tells me of some extraordinary event he has witnessed, I might assent to the proposition that the event did indeed occur, but my assent would be hesitant. In these two types of case it is by natural causal means that the effect, my hesitant assent, is produced. The assent can be thought of as the conclusion of an argument whose premiss is the evidence, whether the perceptual evidence or the word of a self-styled eye-witness. Such assent is 'opinion', in the technical sense of the term employed during the late Middle Ages. The two things that jointly distinguish it from other types of assent are that it is caused by purely natural means and is given hesitantly; hesitantly, because there is sufficient evidence to say 'yes', but not sufficient to ground certainty. We have what was termed a *motivum probabile*, a 'probable motive' for giving assent.

These two sorts of assent, evident assent and opinion, are alike in having a purely natural cause. But in Chapter Three we observed that there is another kind of cause, the act of will, which is distinguished by the fact that it is a form of free cause. What distinguishes the free cause from the natural is that whereas the effect of a natural cause happens necessarily, in the sense that in the very same circumstances in which that effect is produced there could not have been a different effect instead, the effect of a free cause happens contingently, in the sense that in the very same circumstances in which that effect is produced a different effect could have been produced instead. Since there are these two sorts of cause, the natural and the free, a question arises whether assent must have a natural cause or whether it can have a free cause. John Mair and his circle had a good deal to say in this area – unsurprisingly since it defines the space within which faith can breathe. Their answer is that the assent of faith is an assent freely given; that is, it is *willed*. Scotus had already demonstrated that many acts of mind are subject to will, and had pointed out that it is this fact that permits the conclusion that it is possible to sin in thought, no less than in word and deed. What is here at issue is the fact that among the mental acts that are subject to will is our assent.

It was (and is) held by the Church that certain acts of assent are meritorious. These acts concern the truths that save. Let us suppose that acts of assent are in no way subject to voluntary control, but instead are subject solely to natural necessity. In that case we might stand well with the Lord in virtue of performing acts for which we are no more responsible than we are responsible for the colour of our eyes. We did not will either to give an assent of faith or to have blue eyes. We assent and we have blue eyes by natural necessity. And –

something truly terrible – we might stand ill with the Lord for not giving an assent of faith, and this despite the fact that not giving it was not subject to our voluntary control. For those for whom there would be a deep injustice in a world in which one could stand well or ill with the Lord on account of something over which one had no voluntary control, the position of the medieval Church would provide some comfort, though only some. For the Church taught then, as it teaches now, that an assent of faith is freely given.

One aspect of this teaching is the Church's declaration, as often ignored in practice as maintained in theory, that faith cannot be forced or compelled. St Augustine knew the teaching far better than did many who believed themselves his followers. John Mair, who really was a follower of St Augustine, quotes him as saying: 'Someone can enter a church while willing not to. He can approach the altar while willing not to. He can receive the sacrament while willing not to. But he cannot believe unless he wills to.' (Mair, *In 1 Sent.* fol.1 *verso*) A victim can be frogmarched up the aisle and baptised against his will; he can even be frightened into a declaration of faith. But of course, to be willing to declare that one believes is not the same as to believe. Real belief, an inner assent of faith, is willed or it is nothing. The point matters to Mair, whose *History of Greater Britain* contains a number of references to the Church's malpractice in respect precisely of acts pertaining centrally to the faith. And so we find him arguing: 'Since God obliges us to believe, and does not oblige us to do that which surpasses our powers, believing will be a free act and so will not believing.' To which he adds: 'Nothing is a precept unless the will cooperates in its fulfilment.' Plainly Mair was determined not to be misunderstood on this matter; what was at issue was too important for this faithful son of the Church who believed that his Church had too often been unfaithful to itself.

Yet what are we to do? How are we to accomplish an assent of faith? At first blush the idea of *willing* to give assent to a proposition seems bizarre. I cannot will to assent to the proposition that the paper is yellow if I can see that it is white, or will to assent to the proposition that the sound is mellifluous if I hear that it is harsh. The evident assent to the proposition affirming the whiteness of the paper or the harshness of the sound is an insurmountable obstacle to an assent of faith to the proposition that the paper is yellow or to the proposition that the sound is mellifluous, for such an assent of faith would contradict the evident assents that are naturally caused by our senses, and are therefore unshakable. However, Mair and his colleagues, such as Lokert and Crab who also wrote on this topic, were not thinking about willing assent to propositions concerning things regarding which we have the overwhelming evidence of our senses. There is nothing we can do about propositions to which we give evident assent except perhaps avert our gaze or stop up our ears, so that the evidence on the basis of which we gave our evident assent is no longer present to us. Mair and his friends had a different starting point, namely opinion, an assent given on the basis of evidence which is sufficient to support hesitant assent, and nothing more than hesitant assent. The assent is therefore not irrational, for there is evidence to support it. At this point the will can come into play.

Consider for example the evidence of an eyewitness. His testimony is not by itself sufficient to produce unhesitant assent. He might be lying, or joking, or be plain deceived, but he is probably reporting what actually happened so we say 'yes', but hesitantly. The situation is common enough. But sometimes we advance from that position. We decide to take the person's word for it, to trust him and not simply say 'yes' hesitantly. We can of course give hesitant assent merely on the balance of probabilities – for by and large it is our experience that people tell the truth. However, I am not now speaking about the balance of probabilities, but about an assurance which is a product of a decision we have taken to commit ourselves to the person's probity. I am not saying it is reasonable to make such a commitment; I am simply saying that it is a matter of common experience that we often do make one. To do so is to give an assent of faith.

We should bear in mind that this analysis by John Mair and his colleagues applies not only to religious faith, but also to faith that we have in people, ordinary people, friends and otherwise. This concept of assent can be brought to bear in the description of most sorts of human relations. Such assent is in the interstices of our living, and it is hard to imagine how human society could maintain itself in a recognisably human form if we were not forever giving assents of faith, and having our word accepted on faith. The concept expounded by Mair and his friends relates directly therefore to a central feature of human life, a feature without which a properly human life would hardly, if at all, be possible, and would hardly, if at all, be worth living.

I should like to make a clarificatory point here that has to be pressed home in light of the importance that John Mair and his colleagues attach to the concept of an assent of faith. For there is a line of thought developed by Scotus that appears to be tailor-made for the concept of assent of faith; and I wish to argue that in this case appearances are deceptive. Seeing why they are deceptive will give us a firmer hold on the concept.

We recall that Scotus attends to human will with respect to its power to affect our judgments. So, for example, I am engaged in a dalliance which I judge, though hesitantly, to be improper. This judgment of mine should be classed as an opinion. But I prefer not to settle for having a mere opinion on this matter. The situation calls for a tougher form of judgment. So, by an act of will, I focus upon the inner aspect of the dalliance and come to see that at its heart is an act of treachery. My hesitant assent is thereby transformed by an act of will into an unhesitant assent to the proposition that my behaviour is morally outrageous. Yet this is not a case of opinion becoming an assent of faith, despite Mair's doctrine that an assent of faith is a joint product of an opinion and an act of will. Let us consider the case of my opening my eyes by an act of will and seeing a red-backed book right there in front of me. I had put it there half an hour earlier before falling asleep. I wake up with an opinion that there is a red-backed book there, because I vaguely remember putting it there shortly before. And then by an act of will I look, and I confirm what I had opined. It is the same proposition as the one to which I had just previously given hesitant assent, namely that there is a red-backed book there, but I have moved from opinion to evident assent. And yet the will was involved. Whether a move is from opinion to assent of faith, or from opinion to evident assent, depends on the contribution made by will. In the case of seeing the book the act of will merely put me in a position to make the evident assent. For once I have opened my eyes natural causality takes over and necessitates my seeing what I see, and necessitates my consequent judgment that the book is right there. In the case of my judging that my dalliance is really an act of treachery, by an act of will I have focused upon the moral dimension of the act, and once focused upon it my judgment is made by natural necessity. The opinion that I am behaving badly is transformed into an evident assent to the same proposition. This is therefore not an assent of faith. There is no question here of *willingly committing myself* to the truth of the proposition. At that final stage the will is simply not engaged. It has already done its job by getting me to focus on the central moral feature of the case. Thereafter natural causality determines the outcome, namely an evident assent.

Once an assent of faith is made we cannot sit back smugly, assured that the assent will stay in place. The gaining of faith is a holding operation; once gained, the position may have to be defended. This is not to say that once an assent of faith has been made it has to be made again and again. Such a picture does not correspond in the least to the ordinary familiar facts. George Lokert addresses this matter. He affirms that an assent of faith has two causes. One of them is the premiss which forms the basis of our opinion that a given proposition is true. The other is an act of will by which we will to adhere firmly to that proposition and will not to seek reasons for accepting an opposing position. (*Scriptum* sig.f 5 *recto*)

Two points follow from this doctrine. One is that on this account of an assent of faith, such assent is never irrational, for the proposition to which the assent of faith is given must first occur as the conclusion of an argument whose premisses are sufficiently strong to permit one to hold an opinion that the conclusion is true. The second point is the recognition that an assent of faith can always be revised. The assenter does not reject out of hand the possibility that he might happen upon evidence which conflicts with his faith. What he is saying is that he is not going to seek out such evidence. If he comes across it, then so be it; he will respond. But meantime, having made his commitment, he will get on with his life on that basis. This account of the matter seems to me to be firmly rooted in experience of how people actually do lead their lives. It is good philosophy and, as such, maintains a strong grip on what we all think of as reality.

CHAPTER 6

On being sceptical

The concept of sense was investigated by the philosophers of the Scottish Enlightenment. The first great philosopher of the period, Francis Hutcheson, examined the concept, and his position was widely influential, even if not always accepted. In this chapter I shall briefly consider Hutcheson's account, and shall then present a philosophical position, that of David Hume, that arguably grew out of Hutcheson's, though growing in a direction that seems not to have given Hutcheson great pleasure. Hume's *A Treatise of Human Nature*, in its turn led to three philosophical masterpieces, all by Thomas Reid. In the next chapter I shall focus on doctrines in the first two of these works, An Inquiry into the Human Mind on the Principles of Common Sense (1764) and *Essays on the Intellectual Powers of Man* (1785), leaving till Chapter Eight a consideration of the third work. Reid's doctrines regarding the senses are close in content and spirit to Scotus and Mair, as I hope to make plain.

Hutcheson tells us that sense is 'every determination of our minds to receive ideas independently on our will, and to have perceptions of pleasure and pain'. (Hutcheson, ed. Downie, p.115) There are obscure aspects to this definition, concerning, for example, the precise meaning of 'determination of the mind' and of 'idea', but it should be evident that the territory we are on is the same as the territory on which we were encamped while discussing the pre-Reformation Scots. For Hutcheson is focused on what takes place in the mind and is considering this in relation to acts of will. He evidently wishes to make a distinction between those ideas which are dependent upon will and those which are not, and our ideas of sense are of the independent kind.

By 'ideas' Hutcheson means the contents of our mind, things such as sensations, feelings and thoughts. A bird sings and I have an auditory sensation, an idea of the sound, which is in my mind independently of my will. And if I stop up my ears the auditory sensation ceases, also independently of my will, and dependently upon the physiology of the ear. I touch the table and have a tactile sensation, an idea of the table's firmness and smoothness. This idea, the sensation, likewise is in my mind independently of my will. And when I remove my hand from the table the tactile sensation ceases, also independently of my will, and dependently upon the physiology of the hand. These ideas are to be distinguished from other sorts of ideas, such as thoughts that I conjure up, maintain in existence, and direct, all by an act of will. The contrast is plain. I cannot help seeing what is right in front of me, and neither, while looking at it, can I will it out of existence. In this sense of 'sense' there is a faculty of 'external sense', the sense by which we are determined to have visual, auditory, tactile, gustatory and olfactory sensations. These sensations arise by our nature or by natural causality.

As well as the five external senses, Hutcheson discusses in addition four kinds of sense. Famously one of these is what he terms 'moral sense', the sense by which we perceive virtue or vice in ourselves or others. On observing a given act the idea of virtue or of vice arises in us not by will but by nature. It is as if the moral quality of an act is like the colour of a wall or the firmness of a table. And as the idea of colour or of firmness arises irresistibly in us when our visual or tactile sense is operating in the relevant context, so also the idea of virtue or of vice arises irresistibly in us when our faculty of moral sense is operating in the relevant context, for example, a context in which someone is performing a kindly act or someone is wantonly attacking another person. Hutcheson speaks also of an 'inner sense', by which we perceive such things as beauty, harmony and grandeur.

Some of our ideas of sense are pleasurable and others painful. The ideas of virtue and of beauty are examples of the one kind, and the ideas of vice and ugliness examples of the other. Matching the naturalness of the occurrence of these ideas is the naturalness of desires which arise, or well up, in us. 'From the frame of our nature', in Hutcheson's phrase, there arises a desire for external sensory pleasures, the pleasures of touch and taste, and so on, and an aversion to external sensory pains. From the frame of our nature there arises a desire for virtue and an aversion to vice. Hutcheson is insistent that these things are not subject to voluntary control, nor mediated by a process of reasoning. On the contrary their two chief features are that they are unmediated by premises and that they arise by a process of natural causation. This is not to deny that there is ample scope for the exercise of the will and of reason in the fields of morality and aesthetics. Of course there is such scope. But unless the sight of acts of kindness, generosity, fairness, and so on, produced in us, 'from the frame of our nature', an immediate approval and pleasure, we could not have a recognisably human morality. Likewise unless certain sights, sounds, and so on, produced in us, 'from the frame of our nature', an immediate approval and pleasure, we could not have a recognisably human aesthetic. These feelings of pleasure, and the corresponding feelings of pain in the presence of vice and ugliness, simply well up. They are the voice of nature, as articulated in us, determining our moral and aesthetic values.

There is room for discussion concerning Hutcheson's view of the precise relation between on the one hand the sense of virtue and of beauty, and on the other hand the pleasure we take in virtue and beauty. A feeling or sentiment of pleasure wells up when we see acts of a certain kind and we say that they are virtuous acts. Is there any more to the existence of the virtue of an act than the pleasure that naturally wells up in us when we see it? Likewise, is there any more to the existence of the beauty of a certain painting than the pleasure that naturally wells up in us when we see it? On a common interpretation of Hutcheson, the moral and aesthetic qualities of things can be accounted for in terms of the feelings, or sentiments, that the qualities naturally produce in us 'from the frame of our nature'.

On this basis Hutcheson is commonly regarded as holding a 'sentimentalist' theory of morality and of aesthetics. Such a theory does not imply a denial of the existence of moral and aesthetic qualities, but it does imply that we are wrong to think that these qualities are really in the act of the agent or the painting we are judging rather than being either the sentiments prompted by the act or the painting, or at least a product of those sentiments. It is as if we have the sentiments, the agreeable or disagreeable feelings, and read them as qualities in the agent or the painting. That is, we read the qualities into the agent or the painting though we think that we do no more than find the qualities there. It is possible to interpret the next major development in the philosophy of the Scottish Enlightenment as Hume catching this Hutchesonian ball and running with it. There are other interpretations but the one that I shall be presenting is in the mainstream and is probably the commonest.

Let us make a distinction, one hard to define but easy to grasp in a non-technical way, between on the one hand seeing a dog and on the other hand thinking about a dog though none is present; or between hearing a sound and imagining one; or between feeling fear and afterwards, in a cool moment, thinking about the emotion. The opening pages of Hume's *Treatise* are taken up with this distinction, and since he aims to work the distinction hard he introduces convenient terminology for it. To see a dog is to have an impression of one, to hear a sound is to have an impression of one, to feel anger is to have an impression of anger. On the other hand to think about a dog is to have an idea of one, to imagine a sound is to have an idea of one, and so on. Hume thinks of the idea as a copy or likeness of the corresponding impression.

He lists two criteria for distinguishing impressions from their corresponding ideas. The first is their greater liveliness or vivacity. The second is their temporal priority – the fact that impressions occur first. Hume quickly qualifies this latter point. He distinguishes between those impressions and ideas, such as impressions and ideas of dogs and of tartan rugs, which are complex, and those impressions and ideas, such as of an undifferentiated patch of yellow and of an undifferentiated pure musical note, which are simple. And the doctrine, duly qualified, concerning temporal priority is that every simple idea is preceded by a corresponding simple impression.

However, the first criterion, that concerning greater liveliness, does not always work, since some impressions are so faint that, as Hume admits, we cannot distinguish them from ideas. And conversely an idea may be so lively or vivid as to approach closely the liveliness of the corresponding impression. Neither does the second criterion always work, for, as Hume allows, it is possible to form an idea of a given shade of blue, even though we had not actually seen that shade before. This might appear a minor exception, but it points to the possibility that we can form an idea of a shade of any colour despite not having actually seen that shade before, and can form the idea of a sound, a note, that we have not heard before, and so on for all the sensory modalities. So Hume's small exception is not so lonely. It conflicts with the whole empiricist drive of his philosophy, and a rethink of his second criterion is therefore badly needed. None is forthcoming.

I should like to pursue this point by means of a consideration of both the title and the subtitle of Hume's *Treatise*. The subtitle is: *Being an Attempt to Introduce the Experimental Method of Reasoning into Moral Subjects*. This clause, though commonly ignored, is endlessly interesting; it contains an entire philosophy. As regards the richly suggestive main title, we learn that the subject matter is human nature, and from a Humean perspective this means considering human beings as parts of, or as substances within, the order or system of nature. If, therefore, there is a methodology appropriate for the scientific investigation of nature it follows that that methodology is also appropriate for the scientific investigation of nature in so far as nature is articulated in human beings. But there is an appropriate methodology. It was formulated by Sir Isaac Newton, the hero not only of the Scottish, but also more generally of the European Enlightenment, and at its centre is the idea that scientific progress is made only on the basis of observation and experiment. By means of observation and experiment the scientist works towards a law of nature and then tests the law by further observation and experiment.

The reference, in the subtitle, to the introduction of the experimental method of reasoning into moral subjects indicates the employment of Newton's methodology not, however, in the investigation of dead matter but in the investigation of human nature. But Newton's methodology implies that if a test of a statement of what may be a law of nature produces a result which conflicts with the statement, then something has gone wrong, whether it be the statement, or the test, or something else. Yet, although Hume admits that we can form a simple idea of a shade of blue though we have never previously actually seen that shade, he neither calls into question his supposed law concerning the temporal priority of simple impressions, nor calls into question the possibility of having a simple idea before having the impression. Plainly Hume, who saw himself as 'the Newton of the moral sciences', does not, in this matter, remain faithful to Newton's methodology.

Nevertheless, there is no doubt that Newtonian thinking is never far from the surface of the *Treatise*. Sometimes indeed it sits on the surface, and it is necessary for us to note one such occasion. According to Newton's law of gravity the mutual gravitational attraction of any two particles of matter is directly proportional to the product of their masses and inversely proportional to the square of the distance between them. The law is universal; it applies to every particle of matter. Newtonian particles can be thought of as simple in virtue of the fact that they are impenetrable solids, solids which are so hard that they can never be worn down or broken into pieces.

We have here two concepts, of a particle and of a law of attraction of particles, that Hume deployed. His starting point is the fact that the ideas in our mind are not entirely loose and unconnected, but on the contrary display a measure of uniformity; and his explanation is that there are principles of association of ideas, principles of union or cohesion of our simple ideas, that operate with a 'gentle force' and that 'commonly prevail'. He lists three principles, without a demonstration that the three form an exhaustive list. I think we are facing here an application of the 'experimental method of reasoning'. Hume has examined the contents of his mind and has concluded that there are three and only three principles of association. He would no doubt say that there is no way, other than such observation, by which a correct and exhaustive list could be drawn up.

The three principles are as follows. First, if two things that we have perceived resemble each other, then the idea of one of them will tend to produce an idea of the other. Secondly, if we have perceived two things placed together then an idea of one will tend to produce an idea of the other. And thirdly, if we think that events of kind A cause events of kind B, then the idea of an event of the one kind will tend to produce an event of the other kind. Here we have the three principles of association by resemblance, contiguity and causation, and Hume's comment on them is: 'Here is a kind of ATTRACTION, which in the mental world will be found to have as extraordinary effects as in the natural, and to shew itself in as many and as various forms.' (Treatise, 12-13) The language of 'attraction' is Newtonian, but so also is the entire picture that Hume paints. Hume employs Newtonian space as an analogue for the mind. Just as there are material particles in Newtonian space, so also are there mental particles, simple ideas, in mental space, the mind. And just as there is a law of attraction governing the behaviour of particles in Newtonian space, so there are laws of attraction governing the behaviour of simple ideas in the mind. Simple ideas gravitate towards each other in the mind. Hume does not offer us a mathematical formula corresponding to Newton's inverse square law. Such precision is not achievable. But the parallel is clear: physical space as against mental space (the mind), physical particles as against mental particles (simple ideas), and physical gravitation as against mental gravitation (attraction of ideas). I cannot think what would count as a more Newtonian picture of the human mind. If Hume is not the Newton of the moral sciences then no-one is.

The contents of the mind, on this account, constitute a complex network of causal relations, with ideas causing ideas, by virtue of the relations of resemblance, contiguity and causation. Of these three Hume was particularly interested in the causal relation, and something should be said about his account, which is one of the most dazzling pieces of philosophy of the Scottish Enlightenment. It is the piece of philosophy that Kant described as awakening him from his dogmatic slumbers, and if it had that effect on Kant then all the more reason why we should lay ourselves open to its influence.

The chief focus of Hume's attention in his discussion of causality is the necessary connection between a cause and its effect. If A causes B then B does not happen by chance or merely coincidentally; on the contrary B must happen. Evidently we have an idea of the necessary connection between a cause and its effect. For we are aware of causal relations, and the recognition that A caused B includes the recognition that B happened necessarily. This allows Hume to bring to bear his doctrine that impressions are temporally prior to ideas. If we have an idea of a necessary connection, then presumably we have had an antecedent impression of a necessary connection.

Well, have we? We see the cause and effect, say the golf club hitting the ball and the ball leaving the tee, but do we also see the necessary connection between cause and effect? Do we ever see necessity? If I restrict myself to describing what I see, then I must describe only the club hitting the ball and the ball moving away. I see what happens but not the necessity of what happens, even though I might believe that what happens to the ball is necessary. Nor apparently are my other senses of help. If I do not see the necessity, then even less do I hear it, or touch it, and so on. It was Hume's belief that necessity is not available for inspection by our five external senses. Perhaps then it is a mistake to think that the necessity that relates an external cause to its external effect is itself external, even if it is natural to think that it is external. But observation does not reveal necessity out there, and perhaps therefore we have to look elsewhere. That is what Hume does.

Suppose two substances, A and B, which are of a kind unknown to us. We observe that A touches B and that B immediately turns green. Is B's behaviour coincidental or is it caused by A's contiguity? Suppose that we again observe that A touches B and that B immediately turns green. At the point at which we decide that contact with A causes B to turn green, we expect B to turn green on contact with A. The expectation is the crucial new feature. The expectation is analysed by Hume in terms of a lively idea that we form of B immediately turning green when we have an impression of A touching B. We do not reason from A's touching B to B's changing to green. Reason plays no part in this process. Instead a custom or habit of mind comes into play; so often have we seen contact between A and B followed immediately by B's turning green, that the next time we observe the contact we immediately, by a custom or habit of the mind, form a lively idea of B turning green. We do indeed have an idea of necessary connection, and we do have an impression of it also, but the necessity is not where we naturally suppose it to be. It is not where A and B are, but in our minds, in the form of the determination of the mind to form a lively or vivid idea of B as soon as we see A. What seems to be on the outside thus turns out on analysis to be on the inside. But the expectation is, so to say, read into the world and regarded by us as a feature of the world when it is we who are seeing the world in terms of something that is, and can only be, in the mind.

There are many sorts of thing that we suppose to be in the 'real' world, the world outside our mind. We think that other people, chairs and tables, planets and suns, and so on, are 'real' in the sense that they are external to and independent of us, and that therefore they and their attributes do not depend upon an act of our mind for their existence. If we ceased to exist they would continue to be as we believe them now to be. Among the things that we suppose to be real, in the sense just sketched, is the necessity of the relation between causally related things. That is, we do not suppose that we are responsible for the causal relations between things in the real world, nor therefore for the fact that when an event happens in the real world its effect must happen or necessarily happens. To accept this metaphysical view is to be a 'realist' about causal necessity. Hume, as we have seen, is sceptical about realism in respect of causal necessity, and adopts a nominalist position instead. A nominalist holds, as regards something that is generally supposed to exist in the real world and to be external to and independent of us, that it is really in our mind or is a product of a mental act.

This situation is very similar to the one we found in Hutcheson's philosophy, as regards moral and aesthetic qualities. On the common interpretation of Hutcheson that I expounded earlier, he was nominalist, not realist, about virtue and beauty. For on that interpretation, he holds that things we naturally suppose to be on the outside, the virtue of an act we are looking at and the beauty of a painting, are to be analysed in terms of a feeling that wells up in us from the frame of our nature. According to Hume, likewise, on observing a repeated sequence of X followed by Y, there wells up in us, from the frame of our nature, an expection of Y, a feeling that Y will occur, next time we observe X. It is as if Hume has taken Hutcheson's sentimentalist account of moral and aesthetic qualities and applied it to causality.

We might wonder how much more of the external world is really owing to us. Hume thinks that almost all of it is. I shall now turn to this doctrine.

Yet how can he believe this, that there are no other people, nor chairs and tables, planets and suns? But Hume does not say this. His point is that these things exist, but that they do not continue to exist when not present to our senses nor do they have an existence distinct from us. These real things, believed by us to be able to get along nicely without us, are, to use Hume's own term for them, 'fictions', that is, things that have been made by us, in large measure a product of our imagination.

Hume affirms: 'We may well ask, What causes induce us to believe in the existence of body? but 'tis vain to ask, Whether there be body or not? That is a point, which we must take for granted in all our reasonings.' (*Treatise* p.187) His position is that the senses cannot give rise to our notion that external bodies that are independent of us exist when they are not being sensed. To believe that the senses can give rise to the notion is a contradiction, for to know whether bodies are still there we would need to use our senses and in that case the bodies whose existence we discover would not be unsensed bodies. Nor can the faculty of reason give rise to this notion, for reason could do so only by producing valid arguments to support the conclusion that there are bodies that exist external to, and independent of, us. But there are no such arguments, and even if there were they would no doubt be so abstruse that most people could not grasp them, and so could not be using them as the basis for their belief in the existence of continued external bodies. The only faculty left that could give rise to the notion is imagination. And much of Hume's dazzling discussion on our perception of the external world is devoted to showing how imagination works on the chaotic swirl of impressions and ideas to produce our notion of an external world populated with things that are independent of us, and distinct from us. We read our impressions and ideas and, in doing so, we read into them, with the aid of imagination, a coherence and continuity that they do not have in themselves.

The product of this exercise of imagination is our world. We are world makers, creating our world on the side without even noticing what we are doing. This is nominalism on a heroic scale. First we learn that the necessary connection that exists between a cause and its effect is a product of a mental act, owing its existence to a habit of mind to believe in the existence of the second event when we perceive the first, and then we learn that the events themselves, the causes and the effects, are also products of a mental act, an act that creates coherence and continuity out of the chaotic swirl of ephemeral impressions and ideas.

We find in this stage of Enlightenment philosophy a process of internalisation. It begins with Hutcheson and reaches its terminus with Hume. First, moral and aesthetic qualities are said to be on the inside, existing in the form of sentiments or feelings, then the necessary connections between causes and effects are said to be on the inside, and then the causes and effects themselves are also said to be on the inside. It is difficult to see how the process of internalisation could be carried much further. It was at this point that the reaction set in. In the judgment of Thomas Reid, Hume's philosophy had the logical form of a *reductio ad absurdum*. Logic teaches us that if a set of premisses yields an absurd conclusion, then at least one of the premisses has to be rejected. Reid believed that he had discovered which of Hume's premisses had to go, and he spent the rest of his life working out the implications of that piece of knowledge.

CHAPTER 7

On being sensible

At the basis of Hume's philosophy is the theory of ideas, a doctrine nowadays associated especially with René Descartes, John Locke, Bishop George Berkeley and David Hume, though many other philosophers embraced it in one or other of its forms; indeed it was part of the common philosophical currency of the age. According to the theory of ideas, on Reid's understanding of it, the immediate objects of knowledge are ideas in our mind, and it is through our knowledge of ideas that we know things in the external world. We know from Reid's own testimony that in his early years he was an adherent of the theory. In 1785 he wrote: 'I once believed this doctrine of ideas so firmly as to embrace the whole of Berkeley's system in consequence of it.' (*Essays on the Intellectual Powers* p.283A), and in the same place he informs us that he began to question the doctrine more than forty years previously. Elsewhere he affirms: 'I never thought of calling in question the principles commonly received with regard to the human understanding, until the *Treatise of Human Nature* was published in the year 1739.' (*Inquiry* p.3) It was therefore Hume's *Treatise* that awoke Reid from his dogmatic slumbers. However, though an important part of Reid's philosophy is negative in so far as it is a destructive attack on Hume's development of a particular version of the theory of ideas, he also makes a significant positive contribution to philosophy, particularly in his discussions of perception and of human action. We shall consider these various matters in turn. First the critique of Hume.

As we saw in Chapter Six, Hume mentalised everything. Impressions and ideas are contents of the mind and all else is constructed out of them. It is none the less possible to distinguish within Hume's philosophy between mental things and material things, but everything falls under the heading of 'mental'. Material things are really mental, according to Hume, and we naturally think otherwise only because we cannot help reading our impressions and ideas in such a way as to perceive some things as independent of, and distinct from us. That Hume sees everything as mental is paradoxical since, as we observed, his model for mind was material, namely Newtonian space, containing simple solids, particles of matter, whose behaviour is determined by a principle of association, the law of gravity. This model works so hard in Hume's system that it is necessary to determine whether it is a suitable model. Reid however believed that a material model of mind, any material model, not only the Newtonian, is bound to fail. Mind is far too different from matter for matter to serve as an appropriate model for mind.

But a model for what? What is mind? Reid asks himself this, and gives up almost at once: 'If it should be asked, What is mind? It is that which thinks. I ask not what it does, or what its operations are, but what it is. To this I can find no answer; our notion of mind being not direct, but relative to its operations.' (*Essays on the Active Powers*, p.513A) Some years earlier he had written: 'By the mind of man, we understand in him that which thinks, remembers, reasons, wills.' (*Essays on the Intellectual Powers*, p.220B) Yet Reid, who says this much about mind, says he can find no answer to the question what it is. This is because any account that can be given of it must be in terms of what it does. What can be said about it is that it is of such a nature, or has such an essence, that it can perform acts or operations such as thinking, reasoning, and so on. But the question is left hanging: what properties must mind itself have for it to be able to act in these various ways? This is the question to which Reid finds no answer. Plainly mind is to be thought of as a kind of agent, for it is able to perform acts of various sorts, and it is agents that perform acts. But the question remains: what qualities does mind have, *qua* agent, that permit it to perform such acts as thinking, imagining, conceiving, and so on?

He compares the situation with a library book whose classification number enables the librarian to distinguish it from all the other books in the library and to find it, and yet all he knows about the book is where it is in relation to all the other books in the library. He knows neither the author, nor the subject matter, nor its size, and so on. He has a relative, not a direct notion of it. In somewhat the same way we have a relative, not a direct notion of mind, our knowledge of it being knowledge of it as that which performs such operations as those mentioned earlier. Yet we do not believe that there is merely thinking going on, or reasoning, or remembering, and a persuasive philosophy must acknowledge the fact of unitariness in these operations, unitariness at least in the sense that whatever it is that is thinking and reasoning is also that which is remembering, intuiting and willing. Though we do not have direct knowledge of what it is that is doing all these things, we acknowledge that there is such a thing by our use of the pronoun 'I'.

Hume, introspecting, and finding mental acts of various sorts, but not finding an impression of that which is performing these acts, concludes that mind is nothing more than the bundle of mental things, the impressions and ideas, that we find when we look within. But Hume gives no account of what it is that ties the bits into a bundle and thereby gives the bundle its unity. Reid can reply that the fact that we do not have direct knowledge of something, for example, direct knowledge of what ties the bundle of mental acts, does not imply that we can form no idea of it at all. Indeed we must have some idea of mind if we are to be able to say, after a search, that we have not found an impression of it. An impression of what? Of something corresponding to our idea. We must therefore have an idea of mind if we are even to begin the search. And we do have such an idea. It is something which thinks and imagines and so on. Imperfect as the idea is, and relative as it is to the acts or operations of mind, it is enough to permit us to start searching, and to start rejecting.

One candidate that can be rejected outright is body. Body is extended, solid, and divisible, and it behaves according to Newton's three laws of motion and the law of gravity. In Newton's system material objects are totally passive, inert. A body moving in a straight line will continue to do so forever unless a motive force compels it to change direction, and once its direction is changed, it will continue to go in a straight line in that new direction until a force impressed upon it forces it to change direction again. Material objects cannot initiate anything. There could hardly be a greater contrast than that between minds and material objects, the former as principles of activity and the latter as principles of passivity. Thus, on Reid's account the mind is utterly different from the Humean mind; on the one hand a principle of agency, and on the other hand a mental space in which mental particles, ideas, attract each other according to various principles of association. From a Reidian perspective it seems that when Hume came to the study of mind, he was already loaded with a theory, the Newtonian, and did not see that what he was theorising about, the mind, was of such a nature that nothing that really mattered about it, its metaphysical status as an agent, could be accommodated to the theory.

The term 'in' needs watching. It seems innocent enough. Evidently it signifies a containment relation, for example the relation between a pocket and the pen that is in it. Since we can have thoughts in our mind, there is presumably a containment relation between the mind and the thought. But there is not. A thought is not in my mind in anything like the sense in which a pen is in my pocket. For a thought to be in my mind is for me to be thinking. The mind in which is the thought is therefore not the *container* of the thought but its *agent*, that which is doing the thinking. In so far as 'in' primarily signifies the relation of containment, it tends to reinforce a Newtonian account of the relation between a mind and its thoughts, with thoughts as mental particles in mental space. Reid provides powerful arguments from the direction of common sense against that account.

In the whole of Hume's *Treatise* no concept works harder than that of an idea. Against Hume and all other philosophers who embraced the theory of ideas Reid levels the criticism that ideas, at least ideas in the philosophical sense of the term, do not exist. There is a common and perfectly innocent use of the term 'idea', according to which to have an idea about something is to be thinking about it, or conceiving or imagining it, and so on. But this is not the philosophical use. The common philosophical position concerning ideas is that they are the immediate objects of our acts of thought, and through our knowledge of these ideas we come to a knowledge of what it is that the ideas are ideas of. Thus it was held that it is through our knowledge of the ideas of external things that we come to a knowledge, which is therefore indirect, of the external things themselves. Likewise, it was held that there are past events that we have experienced and that produced in us ideas of them, mental representatives of things distant in time; and it is through our knowledge of the present ideas that we come to a knowledge, which is therefore indirect, of the past events themselves. Such is memory.

The sceptical implications of such doctrines were considered in Chapter Four. The form is the same whether we are considering sensory perception or memory, or any other faculty that is supposed to enable us to get outside our minds. If our knowledge of external things is only ever indirect, mediated by knowledge of ideas, then how can we be sure that the external things are really as we think they are, and how can we be sure that there are any external things at all? And if our knowledge of past events is only ever indirect, mediated by knowledge of present ideas, then how can we be sure that the past events were really as we think they were, and how can we be sure that there were any past events at all? Reid deals with the sceptical implications of the theory of ideas by saying that if a set of premisses implies an absurdity, it is necessary to jettison one of the premisses; and the premiss he jettisons is the proposition that there are ideas, that is, ideas in the philosophical sense. Ideas, according to

Reid, are a philosophical fiction, invented to do a job that they fail to do. Ideas are not objects in the mind that the mind comes to know and through a knowledge of which we come to know the external things. Ideas are, instead, the mental acts through which we reach out directly to external things, and to past events.

Hume, though seeing himself as the Newton of the moral sciences, was not, in Reid's view, Newtonian enough, for Hume failed to pay sufficient attention to the phenomena, in this case the mind and its operations. Close observation, or even not so close, would have revealed that the mind is a principle of action, and that the proper model for mind is an agent and its acts. Hume effected a grand simplification in his presentation of mind in terms of Newtonian space, Newtonian particles, and gravitational attraction – 'simplification' because the same general picture applies to both the outer world and the inner. But to simplify is not virtuous when it leads to falsification, as it does in this case. The mind that discovered the three laws of motion and the inverse square law could hardly have been more different than it was from the world that is bound by those laws.

Reid, finding Hume's conclusions incredible, seeks to remind us of the dictates of common sense. There are certain beliefs that we have by the original constitution of our nature, beliefs that are as much a part of our human nature as is our biological makeup. We cannot prove them, but on the contrary need them if we are to prove anything whatever. The beliefs which are termed 'principles of common sense' include the following: (1) The operations of our mind of which we are conscious really exist, and the best possible evidence for them, for the acts of thinking, imagining, doubting, and so on, is simply that the thinker is conscious of them. (2) We know the past by memory. Of course, memory can deceive us, but if we did not put our faith in it we could never be deceived by anything; even less could we find out that we were ever deceived. (3) 'The thoughts I am conscious of, or remember, are the thoughts of one and the same thinking principle, which I call myself or my mind... Every man of sound mind, finds himself under a necessity of believing his own identity, and continued existence. The conviction of it is immediate and irresistible.' (*Essays on the Intellectual Powers*, pp.231B-232A) (4) Every act or operation supposes an agent. (5) Every quality supposes a subject that has the quality.

Though, according to Reid, these, and the many other principles of common sense, cannot be proved, it can at least be proved that they are principles of common sense. Two sorts of proof are routinely presented by Reid. One sort is linguistic, and the other is practical. As regards the linguistic evidence, Reid holds that our language reflects our beliefs about the world, and the fact that all languages share given features reflects the fact that there are beliefs that are universally held. The universally held belief that all qualities are qualities of something is reflected in the fact that all languages have nouns and adjectives, with the adjectives qualifying the nouns. Likewise the universally held belief that every act is performed by an agent is reflected in the fact that every language has verbs in the active voice and such verbs have a subject term. Whether Reid is correct in his claim that all languages share given syntactic features is a matter for dispute, though the sheer widespreadness of those syntactic features is highly suggestive of common ways of looking at the world.

The second of Reid's criteria for identifying principles as principles of common sense is the practical one already hinted at. People reveal in their behaviour their assent to the principles. By our dealings with people we show that we believe in, for example, the continuing identity of selves through time. It is evident, from my conversation with someone, that I regard myself as the same person who had previously spoken with that same person. Reid sums up his position in this way: 'we may still inquire how the rest of mankind... have got so strong and irresistible a belief, that thought must have a subject, and be the act of some thinking being; how every man believes himself to be something distinct from his ideas and impressions –

something which continues the same identical self when all his ideas and impressions are changed. It is impossible to trace the origin of this opinion in history; for all languages have it interwoven in their original constitution. All nations have always believed it. The constitution of all laws and governments, as well as the common transactions of life, suppose it.' (*Inquiry* p.36; *Enquiry* (Hamilton ed.) p.110A-B)

In the same vein one response to the sceptic who rejects the common sense principles is that the sceptic's behaviour belies his alleged beliefs. Reid affirms: 'It is one thing to profess a doctrine of this [sc. the sceptical] kind, another seriously to believe it, and to be governed by it in the conduct of life. It is evident that a man who did not believe his senses, could not keep out of harm's way an hour of his life; yet in all the history of philosophy, we never read of any sceptic that stepped into fire or water because he did not believe his senses, or that showed, in the conduct of life, less trust in his senses than other men have.' (*Essays on the Intellectual Powers*, p.259B)

The common sense principles that Reid presents are therefore demonstrably universal in the sense of being common to humankind. Though they are incapable of proof, that does not matter; people do not look for a proof of propositions that in any case they cannot help accepting. The only exception to this is the philosopher with a sceptical cast of mind. But the sceptic's position is unlike the common sense position in the sense that common sense and not scepticism is the default position. Philosophical scepticism is, precisely, scepticism about common sense. The onus of proof lies not with the holders of common sense but with those who reject it. Reid claims that the sceptic, one who is sceptical about the claims of common sense, cannot give a coherent account of his scepticism and cannot give any account of anything without presupposing the common sense principles that he seeks to reject. That is, the sceptic, for all his protestations, is as common sensical as the rest of us, for common sense is an original human endowment, part of the constitution of our nature. In one respect, the sceptic's testimony to the truth of common sense is all the more impressive, because even while seeking to show its lack of rational credentials he demonstrates his dependence on that same common sense, by living his life on the assumption that his natural faculties, such as his external senses, are reliable, and do not systematically deliver up fictions.

CHAPTER 8

On being free: Enlightenment perspectives

During the Middle Ages there was extensive discussion of free will. In Chapter Three we saw something of Duns Scotus's contribution to that discussion. Particular matters of concern included both the nature and also the existence of free will. These two big questions, 'What is it?' and 'Do we have it?' were no less prominent in the philosophy of the Age of Enlightenment, and the discussions of the later period matched those of the earlier in many ways. During the Middle Ages there were worries about the reality of free will on account of at least two utterly different sorts of considerations. One was that if the intellect determines the will to act, then the will is not really free. The other was that if God, who is omniscient, knows from all eternity exactly what we are going to do then we are bound to do what he always knew we would, and in that case none of our acts is free. During the Scottish Enlightenment both of these considerations came into play in one form or another. But something, new in formulation even if ancient in origin, had to be faced by the later philosophers writing on free will. After Newton philosophers could not discuss free will as if Newton had not spoken. Certainly Hume could not, and here I shall say something about the Newtonianism of Hume's doctrine of freedom before going on to describe the common sense reaction to that doctrine.

If the mutual gravitational attraction of any two particles of matter in the universe is directly proportional to the product of their masses and inversely proportional to the square of the distance between them then the future behaviour of every particle of matter is absolutely determined by the present position and motion of particles in the universe. Hence, given knowledge of the present position and motion of all the particles, Newtonian mechanics enables us to predict with absolute certainty the behaviour of every particle. If Hume is indeed the 'Newton of the moral sciences' is he therefore a strict determinist in his account of human action? I believe the answer is 'yes'. On the other hand, a cursory reading of the *Treatise of Human Nature* may well suggest that he is not, for he accepts that we are free and he has a good deal to say about the nature of our freedom. How can a strict determinist also hold that we are free? The question is an important one, and the answer points to a formidable unity in the philosophy of the *Treatise*.

As regards the outer world, the world to which Newton's laws apply, Hume is totally deterministic. He writes: ''Tis universally acknowledg'd, that the operations of external bodies are necessary, and that in the communication of their motion, in their attraction, and mutual cohesion, there are not the least traces of indifference or liberty. Every object is determin'd by an absolute fate to a certain degree and direction of its motion, and can no more depart from that precise line, in which it moves, than it can convert itself into an angel, or spirit, or any superior substance.' (*Treatise* pp.399-400) The question arises therefore whether human behaviour is, in relevant respects, sufficiently like the behaviour of outer objects for it to be appropriate to conclude that human beings are no less determined than are Newtonian particles.

In light of the fact that Hume models his account of mind on Newtonian mechanics, we are entitled to suspect that Hume will say 'yes' to this question. Speaking generally for the moment, the outer acts that we perform are a consequence of acts or events in our minds. In Humean terms they are effects of our various feelings and thoughts, impressions and ideas. Hume, as we have already observed, describes these mental things in Newtonian terms, for simple ideas gravitate one to another by principles of attraction which are gentle forces. And this attraction, he tells us, will be found to have as extraordinary effects in the mental world as in the natural. (*Treatise* pp.12-13) The parallel could hardly be clearer or more clearly signalled.

This is not to say that Hume goes so far as to ascribe a strict determinism in the life of the mind. The principles of association are forces 'which commonly prevail', as contrasted with the law of gravity which prevails always and everywhere. And he affirms that nothing is more free than the faculty of imagination, in its ability to arrange simple ideas in new ways. But Hume's language has to be interpreted with care. He also says that we are free in our outer acts, but the freedom that he ascribes to our outer acts is a freedom within the context of a strict determinism. In a wonderful piece of philosophy Hume seeks to demonstrate that our acts, though free, are also necessary. Consequently when Hume says that our acts of imagination are free, we must enquire whether this is a freedom within determinism or a freedom that excludes determinism. It emerges that Hume believes the actions of the mind to be necessitated and believes the supposed freedom of the mind to be a sham; the appearance of freedom masks a reality that is quite otherwise. But if our outer acts are effects of our inner acts, and the inner ones are not really free, then neither are the outer. Hence determinism prevails.

Yet Hume does not deny that we have a will: 'by the *will*... I mean nothing but *the internal impression we feel and are conscious of, when we knowingly give rise to any new motion of our body, or new perception of our mind.*' (*Treatise*, p.399) Hume has a concept of will according to which it is a mental state, an 'impression of reflexion', intermediate between our emotions or passions on the one side, and outer action on the other, with the emotions producing as an effect the impression which is the will, and the will producing as its effect the outer acts. There is therefore a causal chain which proceeds from emotion to will, and from will to action. And as between any cause and effect there is a necessary connection, so also between our emotions and the will there is a necessary connection, and between the will and the outer acts there is also a necessary connection. Hence we should not suppose that because Hume deploys the concept of will he rejects determinism. Indeed, he embraces it. But all this calls for proof. Why say that our supposedly free acts are necessitated? Hume's answer is that what is sauce to the goose is sauce to the gander. The criteria for necessity in the world of material objects are satisfied also by the world of human action. We have already considered these criteria. One is the *constant conjunction* of pairs of events related as cause to effect. A and B must always be perceived together, and in that order, if they are to be seen as causally related. The second criterion is the *inference* of B from A, that is, the custom or habit of mind to expect B, or to form a belief in B, as soon as A is perceived. We have perceived A followed by B so often that on perceiving A we immediately, and by a custom of the mind, form a lively idea of B. The lively idea is a belief in B's existence. Given this concept of causal necessity, Hume's contention is that human acts, no less than purely physical events, are causally necessitated. Let us consider some of his examples. In a famous passage he writes: 'The skin, pores, muscles, and nerves of a day-labourer are different from those of a man of quality: So are his sentiments, actions and manners. The different stations of life influence the whole fabric, external and internal; and these different stations arise necessarily, because uniformly, from the necessary and uniform principles of human nature.' (*Treatise* p.402) And: 'There is a general course of nature in human actions, as well as in the operations of the sun and the climate. There are also characters peculiar to different nations and particular persons, as well as common to mankind. The knowledge of these characters is founded on the observation of an uniformity in the actions, that flow from them; and this uniformity forms the very essence of necessity.' (*Treatise* pp.402-3)

It might be replied, against Hume, that nobody's behaviour is perfectly constant. People can act out of character; they can surprise us. But this very fact seems to accord with Hume's doctrine. For why are we surprised by what a person does if not because we were expecting something different? And if we had an expectation, how did it arise if not from the fact that we had perceived a uniformity in the person's behaviour, and by a custom of the mind we were expecting him to continue behaving in the same way? If this is correct then we think of human action exactly as we think of the behaviour of dead matter, that is, as having a sufficient uniformity to produce in us a mental custom or habit to expect such and such a piece of behaviour in such and such circumstances. But the necessity we ascribe to the behaviour of dead matter is due to (and for Hume is nothing more than) a custom or habit of the mind by which we are determined to form a belief in the existence of the effect when we observe the cause. If we have a custom of the mind by which we are determined to form a belief in the existence of such and such behaviour by a given person when we observe the person to be in a particular set of circumstances, it follows that we see that person's behaviour also as necessitated, in the same way as we see the behaviour of dead matter as necessitated. And the necessity of the human behaviour has the same source, namely the custom of the mind.

Experience seems to accord with Hume's teaching for we think we know some people well, and part of what it is to know them well is to have an insight into how they will behave in given circumstances. We think that people are predictable, just as we think that dead matter is predictable. Of course sometimes people surprise us, but so also sometimes does dead matter. If a fine bone china plate does not break when it falls we are surprised, because sadly we have had ample opportunity to form a custom of the mind to expect fine bone china to smash when it lands. But we do not suppose that nature does not act by strict necessity if the plate remains intact. We suppose instead that there was some hidden cause determining that outcome – perhaps it was really made of something much tougher than fine bone china, or perhaps the surface on which it landed was not hard and instead the plate landed on a thick pile carpet designed to look like concrete.

In effect Hume is saying that the apparent lack of necessity in our acts is due to the imperfection of our knowledge about the agent or his circumstances, and not at all due to an actual lack of necessity. Had we but known enough we would have been able to predict his

behaviour with the assurance with which we predict the courses of
the planets and the phases of the moon, and relatedly we would have
judged the action of the person to have been as necessary as the
behaviour of the celestial bodies. Indeed we are always predicting
people's behaviour. 'A prince, who imposes a tax upon his subjects,
expects their compliance. A general, who conducts an army, makes
account of a certain degree of courage. A merchant looks for fidelity
in his factor or super-cargo. A man, who gives orders for his dinner,
doubts not of the obedience of his servants.' (*Treatise* p.405) Our
reasoning about people's behaviour is thus shot through with
considerations of causality. The government's imposition of a tax is
the cause, and the citizens' compliant behaviour is the effect; the
general's order is the cause and the soldiers' obedience is the effect;
the merchant's entrusting of a task to the factor is the cause and the
factor's honest compliance is the effect. The criteria that require us
to say that the behaviour of dead matter is necessitated, require us
also to say that human behaviour is necessitated.

The doctrine of liberty, concludes Hume, is absurd in one sense
and unintelligible in any other. The absurd sense is the sense according
to which we act freely when our act is uncaused. A free act, on that
account, is one which is indifferent to everything that happenened
before it and happens around it. It is therefore a random event. But if
a person's acts look random we do not even judge him to be sane,
and are barely tempted to think that he is a free agent. In fact, however,
Hume does allow a sense of freedom which is neither absurd nor
unintelligible. He has in mind our concept of a free act as one not
performed by 'force' or 'violence'. If I am pushed then the movement
of my body is not free, nor is it if I am frogmarched. In these cases I
am forced to do what I do. Free acts are unforced acts. But we fall
into absurdity if, having agreed that our acts are free because they
are unforced, we suppose that to be free is to be uncaused.

Nevertheless we have to respect the facts of experience and in
that case we have to respect the fact that we have a sense of our

freedom in our *feeling* that we could do otherwise. But a distinction has to be made between the agent's view of his own act and the spectator's view of that same act. For even if we do not feel constrained or compelled, a spectator may know what we are going to do, because he has seen us often enough in those same circumstances and always responding in the same way to them. So he has formed a mental habit of expecting our act when he sees us in those circumstances. And there is nothing more to a judgment of causal necessity than that determination of the mind to expect the effect on seeing the cause.

On this interpretation Hume's philosophy is determinist in reality and libertarian in vocabulary. We can retain the language of freedom, but our free actions are as necessary as are the motions of particles of matter in Newtonian space. If we think that liberty implies the ability to perform an act which is not necessitated then we must also think that Humean liberty is bogus, a sham. Here it is useful to remind ourselves of Hume's teaching on the will, an internal impression we feel and are conscious of, when we knowingly give rise to any new motion of our body, or new perception of our mind. It is situated between, on the one side, impressions and ideas and, on the other side, an action, with the preceding impressions and ideas causing the will, and the will causing the act. Hume believes that in respect of necessity and causality there is no difference between such a chain of causes and a chain in which domino C fell because domino B fell against it, and domino B fell because domino A fell against it. Hume's description of the *Treatise* as 'an attempt to introduce the experimental method of reasoning into moral subjects' barely hints at the extent to which the *Treatise* Newtonianises moral subjects, and nowhere is the process more dramatic than in the teaching on human freedom. But if Hume is right then our freedom has the same metaphysical status as the external world – it is a fiction.

At the end of Chapter Seven I described common sense principles as the default position. Part of what that means is that common sense does not need to defend its principles, at least as an opening move. The onus is on anyone who does not accept them to argue against them. Only if someone manages to make out a strong case against a common sense principle does common sense philosophy have to swing into action in defence of common sense. Hume has argued that our supposedly free acts are necessitated, as much necessitated as are particles of matter in Newtonian space, and this is as clear a case as could be of an attack on common sense, for if anything is common sense then the fact that we are free is. It is therefore necessary to consider the common sense response to Hume.

Traditionally a distinction has been drawn between active power, which is the power to act on things, as opposed to passive power, the power to be acted upon. Rain has the power (an active power) to extinguish the fire, just as the fire has the power (a passive power) to be extinguished by the rain. But Reid does not like this way of talking about dead matter. Dead matter does not, in his view, have active power, for dead matter, even when the dead matter in question is rain falling on a forest fire, does not have the *power* to do anything nor therefore to put out the fire. Dead matter is purely a principle of passivity. For Reid active power, which is real power, is a power to do and also to refrain from doing. To be unable to refrain is a sign not of power but of powerlessness. In this sense power is to be contrasted with necessity. For what acts from necessity does not have the power not to do what it is doing. That is, it is powerless not to do what it does. If a person is in the grip of an uncontrollable passion, then the resultant act is a sign of utter powerlessness in the face of the passion. The person is so far from being able not to perform the act that it is not even clear that he is the agent. If anything it is more appropriate (or less inappropriate) to think of the passion as the agent for it is the passion that is in control and is determining the act.

It is with such considerations in mind that Reid affirms: 'if the passion be conceived to be irresistible, the act is imputed solely to the passion, and not to the man.' (*Essays on the Active Powers* p.535B)

There is in fact strong reason to believe that Reid does not believe in irresistible passions. I shall return to that point later, but for the present I wish to note his affirmation that 'power to produce any effect, implies power not to produce it'. (*Active Powers* p.523A) This phrase captures a central insight of Reid, and places him in a direct philosophical line to Scotus. For Reid is here speaking of our openness to contraries or opposites, and, as observed in Chapter Three, for Scotus our freedom consists in our openness to opposites, the fact that whatever we do, in the very same circumstances we could have done something different or could even have done nothing at all. Reid holds exactly the same position. To have power is to be able to produce some effect, and also in the same circumstance to be able not to produce it.

Reid is here exploring the common sense concept of freedom, and it is totally un-Humean. Hume sought to locate freedom within a context of necessity, so that the free act, whatever else it is, is also necessitated; the agent could not, in those same circumstances, have done otherwise. Reid holds on the contrary that freedom located within necessity is a counterfeit or spurious freedom. For Reid free actions are contingent; they happen but do not have to: 'It is here very obvious, that a thing may arise from what does exist, two ways, freely or necessarily. A contingent event arises from its cause, not necessarily but freely, and so that another event might have arisen from the same cause, in the same circumstances.' (*Active Powers* p.630A-B) That which is produced by an act which the agent was equally able not to perform in those very circumstances, has contingent existence. Up to the start of the act the product's non-existence was as possible as its existence.

A question arises however concerning the role of passion as a motive to action. Do passions leave us room to act freely? It was Reid's view that passions are resistible: 'We allow that a sudden and violent passion, into which a man is surprised, alleviates a bad action, but if it was irresistible, it would not only alleviate, but totally exculpate, which it never does, either in the judgment of the man himself, or of others.' (*Active Powers* p.575A) Elsewhere he presents a position that is similar though less definite: 'But the madness of a short fit of passion, if it be really madness, is incapable of proof; and therefore is not admitted in human tribunals as an exculpation. And, I believe, there is no case where a man can satisfy his own mind that his passion, both in its beginning and in its progress, was irresistible.' (*Active Powers* p.619B) The role that passions have, one which falls far short of necessitating the will, is that of being incentives to action. Passions give us something to think about, but not necessarily to act on. Nor should we always act on them, and indeed we should never act on them without some regard to wider issues.

The trouble with passions is that they are, in general, totally selfish: 'They draw us towards an object, without any further view, by a kind of violence.' (*Active Powers* p.535A) But we, unlike our passions, have a further view. We consider our good upon the whole (not just the good in relation to a single passion), and we consider also what is our duty. If we do not consider such matters it is not because we are not free to; it is because we choose not to. But in general we do consider them, and in light of them we ask whether it is appropriate to act on a given passion that has arisen. For example, desire for food gives us an incentive to take food that is within reach, but if the food within reach is someone else's then it is wrong to take it without permission. And so we shall, no doubt, refrain from taking it. But though we recognise that theft is wrong, this knowledge no more necessitates our refraining from taking the food than the desire necessitated taking it. Despite the knowledge and the desire we remain free to take and free to refrain. I should like now to pursue this matter further by way of an important distinction that Reid makes between two sorts of motive.

Reid calls them animal motives and rational motives. The former sort, such as dogs and cats might have, include hunger, thirst, cold, and so on. The latter sort include regard for what is for our good on the whole and regard also for what is our duty. Hume, at least on

Reid's (not unreasonable) interpretation of him, sees motives as causes producing acts of will, which in turn produce acts, what we ordinarily call acts. Reid deploys the distinction between animal and rational motives in his discussion of this Humean doctrine, and approaches the matter by way of the question: do people always act on the strongest motive? But what counts as the strongest motive? If we say that it is the one that we act on, then of course people act on the strongest motive. But then the proposition that they do is vacuous.

Let us then work with an alternative account, that of Reid's, namely that the strongest motive is the one that requires most effort if it is to be resisted effectively. We yield to some motives with ease, but to yield to others costs us blood. As regards animals, no doubt they always act on the motive that requires least effort. If their hunger is greater than their thirst, and food and water are equally accessible, they will head for the food first. Certain kinds of consideration, moral or prudential, that would give pause to humans, would not delay an animal. That is to say, we humans may not act on the strongest animal motive in us for we might be swayed by a rational consideration. Though hungry (an animal motive) we may refuse to eat accessible food because we disapprove of theft (a rational motive). In general in humans rational motives are stronger than animal motives, in the sense that when there is a conflict in us between a rational and an animal motive, it is less effort to act according to the rational than according to the animal motive. This is not necessarily to say that it is easier; it might instead just be a bit less difficult. Does the strongest motive always prevail? The answer is surely 'no'. The strongest animal motive does not always prevail in the case of virtuous actions, nor the strongest rational motive in the case of vicious actions.

We are now at the heart of a major issue concerning free will. Given that the strongest rational motive prevails in the case of virtuous action, and the strongest, or commonly the strongest, animal motive prevails in the case of vicious action, what are the implications of this position for determinism? Hume held that we can infer people's actions from their motives, and that sometimes such inferences have a very high degree of probability, as high a degree as we find in inferences concerning the behaviour of dead matter. For example, we infer from the fact that certain people are wise and virtuous that they will do what is their duty or is for their good on the whole, and the vicious and foolish will opt for immediate gratification. Thus Hume.

But it does not follow from this that human behaviour is necessitated. On Reid's concept of free will such a will is open to contraries, so that whatever it is that we do in a given circumstance we could, in that same circumstance, have done something else instead. Let us suppose human beings to be free. What will we do with our freedom? It commonly happens that of the alternative possible acts open to us in a given circumstance one will be seen as giving immediate pleasure, while another (or others) will be seen as being required by duty or as contributing to our good on the whole. The wise and virtuous will opt for duty or the greater good while the foolish and vicious will opt for immediate pleasure. That, then, is what we would do with our freedom. But in fact that is how we do behave. In that case the fact that the virtuous and vicious predictably behave in these various ways is not proof that they are not, after all, free.

Nevertheless, the virtuous do not always act virtuously nor the vicious viciously. Character is not determinative, even if it permits inferences that have a high degree of probability. Being, all of us, free and therefore really open to contraries, the possibility is always available to us to act out of character. Reid's position is unambiguous: 'If we had even the most perfect knowledge of the character and situation of a man, this would not be sufficient to give certainty to our knowledge of his future actions; because, in some actions, both good and bad men deviate from their general character.' (*Active Powers* p.631A)

Of course, Hume would say that if we act out of character that is because there is some new element in the situation that determines us to do so. But Reid would wish to know how Hume knows this. Hume cannot reply that there must be some new element in the situation because every act is fully determined by the antecedent circumstances, and if in what appear to be the same circumstances there is a different act then the circumstances must be different even if we cannot spot the difference. To reply in this way would be to beg the question. For Reid, the question at issue is precisely whether Hume's determinism is correct, and it is not enough simply to assume that it is – for to assume that if the acts are different then so also must be the circumstances is to assume determinism. But if we do not assume determinism and look for the evidence, then what we find is people generally acting in character and sometimes acting out of character and we cannot always find the explanation for this. One possible explanation is that, being free and therefore open to contraries, we can act differently though the circumstances are the same in all relevant respects.

What, then, should be said in response to the doctrine that motives are causes? Reid's reply is that motives should be compared to advice or recommendations, which can be taken up and acted on by the agent and can also be left aside. Likewise, the agent, who will almost always have many motives pushing and pulling in all directions, has to choose from among them, and this he freely does. When the agent takes up a motive, and makes it his own in a special way by acting on it, the cause of the act is not (*pace* Hume) the motive but the agent who has freely acted on that motive. From a Reidian perspective, Hume's chief error in his account of human acts is his omission of the role of the agent. The work that, according to common sense, is done by the agent is, in Hume's system, done by motives. Of course, if Hume fails to take into account the fact that human acts are acts of agents, it is not surprising that he finds no room in his system for the fact of human freedom, however much room he leaves for the vocabulary of freedom. Since I believe that *the* Scottish philosophy is both realist and libertarian, I hold that Reid affirms that philosophy. Indeed, as should by now be plain, I believe he and Duns Scotus to be its greatest representatives.

CHAPTER 9

Why Scottish philosophy matters

This book does not contain a survey, comprehensive or otherwise, of the history of Scottish philosophy. It is directed at the question why Scottish philosophy matters, and an answer to that question does not require a prior survey of the whole philosophical tradition of the country. Instead I have focused upon central features of the Scottish philosophical tradition, in particular its emphasis on realism, or 'common sense'. The realist tradition is particularly strong in its doctrines of freedom of the will, and I have devoted a good deal of space to discussion of writings on free will by Duns Scotus, John Mair and Thomas Reid. Hume also has played a major role in these pages, and is one of the great figures of Scottish culture generally and especially of the Scottish philosophical tradition. But one of my tasks has been to give an account of what has sometimes been called 'the Scottish philosophy', and I believe that Hume worked against rather than with the grain of the Scottish philosophy for, though a Scottish philosopher deeply imbedded within the philosophical culture of this country, he is neither a realist nor a libertarian. On the contrary, what we all like to think of as the real world is, in Hume's view, almost entirely a product of our own imaginative activity. It is, to use his own word for it, a 'fiction'. And in addition he argued strongly for a determinist account of human action even while showing how the language of freedom can be retained.

Nevertheless the Scottish philosophy would be unthinkable without Hume, for since the publication of *A Treatise of Human Nature* it has been difficult, if not impossible, to write philosophy in this country without looking over one's shoulder at him, not simply because he is a figure of universal significance but also because he is a Scottish philosopher. His impact could hardly have been greater in

Scotland, and perhaps one reason for the power and intensity of that impact is precisely that this distinguished son of a distinguished Scottish family wrote so brilliantly against Scotland's prevailing philosophy. Nevertheless, for all his brilliance, he did not attract many disciples, and even less did he found a school of philosophy, certainly nothing remotely to compare with the Scottish common sense school.

His philosophy was not, of course, totally rejected in Scotland. Far from it. His doctrines reappear often and in many guises. To take but one example, in Adam Smith's discussion of the psychology of scientific discovery in his *History of Astronomy* he investigates the sequence: surprise, wonder and admiration. As regards the surprise that leads to scientific discovery, he notes the case in which we observe many repetitions of a pair of events, and then he lets Hume take over. There is, Smith tells us, 'a natural career of the imagination' by which the idea of the first kind of event is followed by an idea of the second kind, and observation of the first kind of event is followed by an idea of the second. As a result of the custom of mind to move from the observation to the idea, the sequence of events seems so natural that we do not wonder why the second kind of event follows upon the first. But when the sequence is broken and an event of the first kind is not followed by its regular partner we are surprised, because a naturally-created expectation has not been satisfied; the 'natural career of the imagination' has been thwarted. Then we wonder why and, with that wonder, scientific investigation begins. This doctrine of Smith's is based very firmly upon Hume's account of causation. Smith's very language indicates the source. Nevertheless this and the thousand other examples that could have been added do not come near to providing support for the claim that there was a school, or nearly a school, of philosophy in Scotland centred on Hume. Nor is there any other reason to believe that there was such a school.

There is an irony in the situation I am describing, the fact that the best known Scottish philosopher of modern times stands out against the centuries-long current of Scottish philosophy. Things have to be held in perspective, however. It is only from an excessively restricted viewpoint that Hume's reputation is seen to be overwhelmingly greater than the reputations of his philosophical contemporaries in Scotland. His greatest opponent, Thomas Reid, was also a towering figure in Scotland in his day and for half a century after his death, and Reid was hugely influential on the continent of Europe, especially in France and Spain, but in Germany also; in addition he had many followers in North America. Several recent studies of his influence indicate a resurgence of interest in his work, and that interest has a strength that derives in part from the fact that it is not only philosophers but also theologians and cognitive scientists who are discovering that Reid had important things to say in their fields, things that sound new and fresh today. The interest in him is anything but antiquarian.

The Scottish philosophy, whose nature I have briefly indicated, is of course part of the wider Scottish philosophical scene, the Scottish philosophical tradition. That tradition is a historically situated enterprise, situated, that is, within the wider culture of Scotland, and it holds a special place in that culture as a principle of unity. One reason why Scottish philosophy matters is precisely that it is, in definable ways, such a principle of unity. I should like to consider this point here.

Philosophy unifies the culture of Scotland by informing almost all aspects of it. Put otherwise, the culture is deeply philosophical. As regards the way in which philosophy informs the culture, some examples, from the thousands readily available, will give an idea of the extent of the role of philosophy. I shall take examples from two of the periods emphasised in this book, the pre-Reformation period and the Enlightenment. Philosophy is found in poetry, prose fiction, law, history, and the empirical sciences. As regards poetry, 'The King's Quair', reputedly by James I (1394-1437), begins with a description of one of the great works of philosophy of the late Roman Empire, *On the Consolation of Philosophy* by Boethius (480-524), and throughout the work the author indicates awareness of medieval philosophy and theology (as well as astrology). Indeed Scottish poetry of the fifteenth and early sixteenth century is replete with philosophical references. No less than 'The King's Quair', and perhaps even more so, 'The Preaching of the Swallow' by Robert Henryson (c.1420-c.1490) calls for a full philosophical analysis. With its opening verses it plunges into one of the great areas of philosophical discussion in the Middle Ages, the extent to which the human intellect is able to form a concept of God. Henryson affirms that our soul is so fettered in its corporeal prison that we cannot clearly understand God, or see him as he is. The philosophical doctrine that our material body is an obstacle to an intellectual grasp of God is then developed in detail in this magnificent poem.

Philosophy is no less present within the poetry of the Scottish Enlightenment. Robert Burns was familiar with *The Theory of Moral Sentiments* of Adam Smith. In that work Smith discusses the problems we face in forming a judgment regarding the propriety of our conduct, and emphasises the role that is played by our imagination in the construction of an impartial viewpoint. As far as possible we should seek to view our acts as an impartial spectator would view them. The concept of such a spectator is deployed at many points, and is in Smith's mind when he writes: 'If we saw ourselves in the light in which others see us, or in which they would see us if they knew all, a reformation would generally be unavoidable. We could not otherwise endure the sight.' (pp.158-9) Burns saw a louse creeping up a lady's bonnet while she was sitting in church, and what he makes of the incident is pure Smith:

> O wad some Pow'r the giftie gie us
> To see oursels as others see us!
> It wad frae monie a blunder free us
>   An' foolish notion:
> What airs in dress an' gait wad lea'e us,
>   And ev'n Devotion!

(To a Louse, stanza 8)

It is hard to believe that Burns did not have Smith's words in mind, but in any case it is clear that Burns' poem can be located very precisely within the philosophy of the Scottish Enlightenment. The same can be said of prose works, such as Henry Mackenzie's *The Man of Feeling* and James Hogg's *Confessions of a Justified Sinner*.

As in poetry and prose, so also in legal writings, philosophy is on or near the surface. Scotland's great writers on law, such as Viscount Stair, Sir George Mackenzie and John Erskine were all well-educated in philosophy, and their philosophy is integral to their writings. Thus, for example, Stair begins his *Institutions of the Laws of Scotland* with sections on justice and law, the law of nature and of nations and the civil law, and this opening to the treatise is as much a work of philosophy as it is a legal work. And Erskine likewise opens his *An Institute of the Law of Scotland* with a distinction that is no less philosophical than it is legal, concerning the term 'law' itself. For as used in such phrases as 'the laws of nature', it signifies 'the settled method of God's providence, by which he preserves the order of the material world in such a manner that nothing in it may deviate from that uniform course which he has appointed for it'. On the other hand, the term, as used in such phrases as 'the law of the land', refers to prescriptions under which we citizens live. These prescriptions can be infringed and infringement lays us open to punishment. It is, of course with such laws, the violable sort, that Erskine is concerned, not with the former, inviolable sort. (*An Institute*, bk.1, title 1, p.1)

Scotland's historians likewise have often been philosophical in their historical writing. Indeed many of Scotland's greatest historians have also been philosophers. During the sixteenth century three major works of history were produced by Scots, Hector Boece, John Mair and George Buchanan, and all three were philosophers no less than they were historians.

David Hume likewise was a historian as well as a philosopher, and indeed in his own day his literary success was due more to his historical writings than his philosophical. But of course he could not write history as if he were not a philosopher with a fully developed system of human nature. He is explicit on the many relations between philosophy and history. For example, he affirms: 'Mankind are so much the same, in all times and places, that history informs us of nothing new or strange in this particular. Its chief use is only to discover the constant and universal principles of human nature, by showing men in all varieties of circumstances and situations, and furnishing us with materials from which we may form our observations and become acquainted with the regular springs of human action and endeavour. These records of wars, intrigues, factions, and revolutions, are so many collections of experiments by which the moral philosopher fixes the principles of his science.' (*An Enquiry concerning Human Understanding*, sect.8, pt.1) This being his position on the relation between history and philosophy, Hume's historical writings could not be other than a philosopher's. And in the next generation, William Robertson, one of the great historians of his age, could not write history as if he were not steeped in philosophy.

Philosophy is also to be found in what we think of as the hard sciences. Colin Maclaurin (1698-1746), who was appointed to the chair of mathematics at Edinburgh University on the recommendation of Newton, turns to traditional philosophical matters during his fullest exposition of Newtonian mechanics, as for example, when he affirms: 'The great mysterious Being, who made and governs the whole system [of nature], has set a part of the chain of causes in our view; but we find that, as he himself is too high for our comprehension, so his more immediate instruments in the universe, are also involved in an obscurity that philosophy is not able to dissipate; and thus our veneration for the supreme author is always increased, in proportion as we advance in the knowledge of his works. As we arise in philosophy towards the first cause, we obtain more extensive views of the constitution of things, and see his influences more plainly.' (*An Account of Sir Isaac Newton's Philosophical Discoveries*, ch.1)

Newtonian mechanics deal entirely with the material world, but Maclaurin holds that our advance in scientific understanding proceeds in tandem with an entirely different advance, in our insight into the beauty and 'contrivance' of things. For Maclaurin the Newtonian world contains particles of dead matter, but it bears witness to the living God. Yet many see science and religion as in mutual opposition, with science giving good explanations in place of the bad ones provided by religious authorities. From the philosophical perspective of Maclaurin, however, there is no fundamental opposition. On the contrary, science points to the reality of a non-natural cause of that natural order which is the object of scientific investigation.

I am speaking here of writings, poetical, legal, historical, and scientific, which are not works of philosophy but which do include passages of philosophical reflection. There are many other writings, historically situated in Scottish culture, in fields such as aesthetics, religion, economics, social theory, politics, linguistics and medicine, in which the authors reflect philosophically upon their culture. And it is also as a form of such reflection that philosophy is a principle of unity of Scottish culture. It provides a framework of concepts and principles in terms of which our culture may better understand itself.

On these grounds I believe that philosophy occupies, and for many centuries has occupied, a central place in Scottish culture. This point is crucial, for nothing sustains a people's sense of cultural identity as much as does its knowledge of its cultural roots. But if knowledge of who we are depends on our knowledge of where, culturally, we are from, then a knowledge of the Scottish philosophical tradition can only help, never hinder, in an understanding of present-day Scotland. Such a historical perspective gives also a sense of the dynamic of the culture, and therefore provides insight into the character of those developments that would go with, and not against, the prevailing ethos. As contributing to such insights, Scottish philosophy now matters greatly to Scotland – as it has always done.

Nevertheless, philosophy, though located within specific cultures, and differing in different places and in different epochs, deals with matters of universal significance. That there is a specifically Scottish philosophy, a historically situated enterprise at the heart of Scottish culture, should not blind us to the fact that Scottish philosophy is part of a philosophical enterprise that is unbounded in time and place.

The philosophy of this country is rooted in world philosophy. It is fed by it and feeds into it, and is one of the great success stories of world culture. It matters to us, and contributing as it still does to the wider philosophical scene, it matters also far beyond Scotland.

Bibliography

Bonansea, Bernardine M., *Man and his Approach to God in John Duns Scotus*, New York 1983

Broadie, A., *George Lokert: Late-Scholastic Logician*, Edinburgh 1983

Broadie, A., *The Circle of John Mair: Logic and Logicians in Pre-Reformation Scotland*, Oxford 1985

Broadie, A., *Notion and Object: Aspects of Late Medieval Epistemology*, Oxford 1989

Broadie, A., *The Tradition of Scottish Philosophy*, Edinburgh 1990

Broadie, A., *The Shadow of Scotus: Philosophy and Faith in Pre-Reformation Scotland*, Edinburgh 1995

Broadie, A., *The Scottish Enlightenment: An Anthology*, Edinburgh 1997

Broadie, A., 'Thomas Reid making sense of moral sense', *Reid Studies*, vol.1, no. 2, 1998, pp.5-16

Broadie, A., 'Scotus on God's relation to the world', *British Journal for the History of Philosophy*, vol.7, 1999, pp.1-13

Davie, George E., *The Democratic Intellect*, Edinburgh 1982

Davie, George E., *The Crisis of the Democratic Intellect*, Edinburgh 1986

Davie, George E., *The Scottish Enlightenment and Other Essays*, Edinburgh 1991

Davie, George E., *A Passion for Ideas*, Edinburgh 1994

Duns Scotus, John, *Opera Omnia*, ed. L. Wadding (Paris: Vives, 1891-95)

Duns Scotus, *Duns Scotus on the Will and Morality*, tr. and introd. by Allan B. Wolter, Washington DC 1986

Duns Scotus, *Duns Scotus Metaphysician*, tr. and introd. by William A. Frank and Allan B. Wolter, West Lafayette, Indiana 1995

Durkan, John and J. Kirk, *The University of Glasgow 1451-1577*, Glasgow 1977

Ferguson, Adam, *An Essay on the History of Civil Society*, ed. Duncan Forbes, Edinburgh 1966

Ferrier, James F., *Scottish Philosophy, the Old and the New*, Edinburgh and London 1856

Haakonssen, Knud, *The Science of the Legislator: The Natural Jurisprudence of David Hume and Adam Smith,* Cambridge 1981
Haakonssen, Knud, *Natural Law and Moral Philosophy, from Grotius to the Scottish Enlightenment,* Cambridge 1995
Henryson, Robert, *The Poems,* ed. Denton Fox, Oxford 1987
Hume, David, *Dialogues Concerning Natural Religion,* ed. Norman Kemp Smith, Edinburgh 1947
Hume, David, *Enquiries Concerning Human Understanding and Concerning the Principles of Morals,* ed. L.A. Selby-Bigge, 3rd ed. by P.H. Nidditch, Oxford 1975
Hume, David, *A Treatise of Human Nature,* ed. L.A. Selby-Bigge, 2nd ed. by P.H. Nidditch, Oxford 1978
Hutcheson, Francis, *Philosophical Writings,* ed. R.S. Downie, London 1994
Ireland, John, *The Meroure of Wyssdome by Johannes de Irlandia,* vol.1 ed. C. MacPherson, Edinburgh 1926; vol.2 ed. J.F. Quinn, Edinburgh 1965; vol.3 ed. C. McDonald, Edinburgh 1990.
Kemp Smith, Norman, *A Commentary to Kant's Critique of Pure Reason,* London 1930
Kemp Smith, Norman, *The Philosophy of David Hume,* London 1941
Kuehn, Manfred, *Scottish Common Sense in Germany,* 1768-1800, Montreal 1987
Lehrer, Keith, *Thomas Reid,* London 1989
Lokert, George, *Scriptum in materia noticiarum,* Paris 1514 (copy in Edinburgh Univ. Lib.)
Maclaurin, Colin, *An Account of Sir Isaac Newton's Philosophical Discoveries,* London 1748
Mair, John, *In primum Sententiarum,* Paris 1519 (copies in Glasgow Univ. Lib and Nat. Lib. Scot.)
Mair (or Major), John, *A History of Greater Britain,* tr. Archibald Constable for the Scottish History Society, Edinburgh 1892
Paton. H.J., *Kant's Metaphysic of Experience,* London 1936
Phillipson, Nicholas, *Hume,* London 1989
Reid, Thomas, *Essays on the Intellectual Powers of Man,* in *The Works of Thomas Reid,* ed. Sir William Hamilton, 6th ed., 2 vols. Edinburgh 1863, (reprinted Bristol 1999), pp.213-508

Reid, Thomas, *Essays on the Active Powers of the Human Mind,* in *The Works of Thomas Reid,* ed. Sir William Hamilton, 6th ed., 2 vols. Edinburgh 1863, (reprinted Bristol 1999), pp.509-679

Reid, Thomas, *Practical Ethics,* ed. K. Haakonssen, Princeton 1990

Reid, Thomas, *Inquiry and Essays,* eds. K. Lehrer and R. Beanblossom, Indianapolis 1975

Reid, Thomas, *Thomas Reid on the Animate Creation: Papers Relating to the Life Sciences,* ed. P.B. Wood, Edinburgh 1993

Reid, Thomas, *An Inquiry into the Human Mind on the Principles of Common Sense,* ed. D.R. Brookes, Edinburgh 1997; also in *The Works of Thomas Reid,* ed. Sir William Hamilton, 6th ed., 2 vols. Edinburgh 1863, (reprinted Bristol 1999), pp.93-211

Ryan, John K. and B.M. Bonansea, (eds.), *John Duns Scotus, 1265-1965,* Washington DC, 1965

Scott, Paul H. (ed.), *Scotland: A Concise Cultural History,* Edinburgh 1993

Scotus, *see* Duns Scotus, John

Smith, Adam, *The Theory of Moral Sentiments,* eds. D.D. Raphael and A.L. Macfie, Oxford 1976

Smith, Adam, *The History of Astronomy,* in *Essays on Philosophical Subjects,* eds. W.P.D. Wightman, J.C. Bryce and I.S. Ross, Oxford 1980

Stewart, Dugald, *The Collected Works,* ed. Sir William Hamilton, Edinburgh 1854

Stewart, M. A (ed.), *Studies in the Philosophy of the Scottish Enlightenment,* Oxford 1991

Tachau, Katherine H., *Vision and Certitude in the Age of Ockham,* Leiden 1988

Thorndyke, Lynn, *Michael Scot,* London 1965

Torrance, T.F., 'La philosophie et la théologie de Jean Mair', *Archives de Philosophie,* vol.32, 1969, pp.531-47; vol.33, 1970, pp.261-93

Torrance, T.F., *The Hermeneutics of John Calvin,* Edinburgh 1988

Wolter, Allan B., *The Philosophical Theology of John Duns Scotus,* ed. M.M. Adams, Ithaca 1990

Index

Other Saltire Publications

Thorbjörn Campbell: *Standing Witnesses*	*0 85411 061 5*
Daiches and Jones (eds): *The Scottish Enlightenment*	*0 85411 069 0*
Johan Findlay: *All Manner of People*	*0 85411 076 3*
John S. Gibson: *Edinburgh in the '45*	*0 85411 067 4*
Ian Grimble: *The Trial of Patrick Sellar*	*0 85411 053 4*
Ian Grimble: *Chief of Mackay*	*0 85411 051 8*
Ian Grimble: *The World of Rob Donn*	*0 85411 062 3*
J. Derrick McClure: *Why Scots Matters*	*0 85411 071 2*
Rosalind Mitchison: *Why Scottish History Matters*	*0 85411 070 4*
David Purves: *A Scots Grammar: Scots Grammar and Usage*	*0 85411 068 2*
Murray Ritchie: *Scotland Reclaimed*	*0 85411 068 2*
Paul H. Scott: *Andrew Fletcher and the Treaty of Union*	*0 85411 077 1*
Paul H. Scott: *Walter Scott and Scotland*	*0 85411 056 9*
Paul H. Scott: *Still in Bed with an Elephant*	*0 85411 073 9*
Paul H. Scott: *The Boasted Advantages*	*0 85411 072 0*

About the Saltire Society

The Saltire Society was founded in 1936 with the aim of protecting and promoting our cultural heritage so that Scotland might once again be a creative force in European civilisation. As well as publishing books the Society makes a number of national awards for excellence in various cultural fields. The Saltire Society has no political affiliation and welcomes as members all who share its aims. Further information from The Saltire Society, 9 Fountain Close, 22 High Street, Edinburgh. EH1 1TF Telephone 0131 556 1836. FAX 0131 557 1675 email saltire@saltire.org.uk Web Site: http://www.saltire-society.demon.co.uk